# JUSTICE DELAYED
## *IS*
# JUSTICE DENIED

*M. Ertuğrul İncekul*

*Translated by*
**Onur Akburç**

**AST** PUBLISHING

**AST** PUBLISHING

# JUSTICE DELAYED
# IS JUSTICE DENIED

*Copyright © AST Publishing, 2023*

All rights reserved.

No part of this publication may be reproduced, distributed, disseminated, stored in a database or information recovery system, in any format or for any purpose, without the
prior permission of the publisher.

This e-book is licensed for your use only.
This e-book cannot be resold or given to others.
If you want to share this book, please purchase a copy for
each individual. If you are reading this book but have not purchased it, or if it was not purchased for your use only,
please return it to the purchaser and buy yourself a copy.

Thank you for respecting the author's work.

www.silencedturkey.org

Published: March, 2023
ISBN: 9798389159167

**Author**
M. Ertuğrul İncekul

**Illustrations**
Nell Berger

**Publication Director**
Ali Topdağ

**Cover & Page Design**
Muhsin Nazif

**Translate**
Onur Akburç

---

**M. ERTUĞRUL INCEKUL** is the founder of cultural, social peace and educational initiatives. He is a member of International Journalist Association in Frankfurt. He has worked as teacher, as educational counselor and as a president of educational institutions in Moscow, Madagascar, Johannesburg, Cape Town, and Europe. He has studied sociology, leadership, social peace, forms of behaviors and organizational skills.

He regularly writes articles in several newspapers and platforms in the fields of literature, culture, sociology, and human rights. He has lectured seminars on the art of living together, ethical values and interaction between different cultures.

He was born in 1973. He graduated from Istanbul Fatih College and İzmir Dokuz Eylül University, studied in the Faculty of English Language Education. He is an educator, an activist, and a writer. He can speak Turkish(native), English, Russian, Portuguese

He's father of Rana, Aydın Yavuz and Mina.

He has two books from Crab Publishing; "Who Would Say?", and "Was it Worth It?"

# CONTENTS

# INTRODUCTION

With its unrestrained and horrendous victimizations, Turkey's State of Emergency period openly demonstrates the reign of a genocide over the previous six years! The events of these recent years, which have been rife with the gravest illegalities in the history of the Republic of Turkey, have been appallingand must be recorded in history. These must be hauled upimmediately and followed up for restitution.

Turkey was already ranked in the global arena with exceedingly poor criteria in terms of democracy and law, and once the patently lawless government declared a state of emergency exploiting the coup attempt as an excuse, the conditions across the country worsened to become further disastrous. Is there any other period when a government squandered so much of the country's resources to further entrench its rule? Is there any other period when the country's people were so decimated? It is impossible to tell, for we are witnessing a period experienced via multiple severe traumas.

Massacring and exterminating people are common genocidal practices. Yet, the state's current stance of physically destroying people with their relatives, children and others through successive pain and agony for years is cruel beyond description. This must be borne in mind evidently.

There is no need to describe these atrocities at length, but what needs to be done is to struggle. Cowering, taking things in stride, fear, hesitation, and surrender must not exist in the textbook of civil society! Several landmark struggles have been given on this matter; yet it is impossible to claim they are sufficient. Those who put up the struggle have done and are doing noteworthy efforts in terms of virtue and human rights, but there is still much more to be done. We will only become a real society when the civil society duly and truly fights against these atrocities! As long as this does not happen, we can only lament this matter, a gesture obviously not of much substance and does not transmute the oppression!

Remembering the agonizing and haunting massacres, prison victimizations, oppression, suffering families; for those who scream "Can anyone hear me?" "Save me!" in the silent dark nights on the waters of the Aegean Sea and Evros River where no one can hear them, and for those who drowned in the waters while crying for help, we all need to uphold the struggle and never give up. It is incumbent to provide unwavering support for all effort done on this matter. The work done so far is insufficient. It is a crucial duty and responsibility to back the hard efforts. Failing to support it is a grave injustice. Make this known to the whole society.

I commend this important endeavour and wish it success in reaching the social awareness it seeks.

**Ömer Faruk Gergerlioğlu HDP Deputy**
*Turkish Grand National Assembly*

***

Nobody is free unless one of us is. That is why, wherever they occur and to whom they are perpetrated, I am worried about human rights violations. Many people must know this for the world to be freer and safer. Intellectuals, authors, civil society leaders and public figures have key roles in raising this awareness. In this sense, I deem my dear friend Ertuğrul İncekul's book immensely precious. It is a bedside book that successfully blends the critical assessments, influential research, historical trends and human rights considerations. It is a must-read for current human rights advocates, aspiring human rights activists, and all concerned by human rights violations.

**Yüksel Kaya**
*Board Member, Solidarity with Others*

My new insights.

I slide foot by foot through time, through space. Occasionally stand still to feel, to slip in the time of oblivion. Then I am picked up by the wind and swirl like a leaf and land somewhere else. I lie still and look at my new environment! At first sight it seems very strange.

I'm a bit in a shock and for a moment I can't breathe. My curious nature prevents me from completely to retire in my cocoon. I inhale very deep, and I must go one to see what is there realy. Then slowly my hart slows down. A warm feeling starts to slip inside my body. It makes me open for myself and you. It has to do with a feeling of love. A love that connects me to you.

I laugh to myself; I laugh about the imaginary bridge that I am crossing.

I'm standing up and I feel that my footsteps are more powerful. At first sight I can't believe this feeling of openness of warmth.

I see you; you see me, we talk....

If we didn't have a feeling of love, I wouldn't meet you. I'm breathing and embrace my new steps.

It isn't easy but with the love in my body I will go step by step and will learn a new language.

No, it isn't easy but in the name of love and connection I have to go on.

**Nell Berger**
*Artist and Performer*

Who is telling the truth and who is not?

As an author and change management entrepreneur, I recently completed my new manuscript, tellingly titled "God's Love and Religions". One chapter in my book concerns Turkish refugees who fled their homeland, Turkey, because of alleged sympathies for the ideas of Muslim cleric and authority Mr Fethullah Gülen.

Once the current Turkish President Erdoğan and Mr Gülen were friends. Now, those inspired by Gülen are detained as terrorists by the current Turkish regime, deprived of what value they possess, socially isolated (read: terrorised) tortured and sometimes murdered. Their status as protected Turkish citizens has been taken away from them and with it their freedom, property, jobs, family harmony and everything else imaginable. Those Turks in the Erdoğan regime's sights (and in doing so, know that many ordinary Turkish residents also participate in this) are rounded up and detained without any legal process (including their wives, children and even their babies). It is barbaric what is going on there in Turkey right now.

Many Turkish residents have seen their terrible fate in Turkey and have fled, often hastily. Many have headed for the West hoping to be safe there, trying to take with them what might still be of interest to them. To make matters worse, the Erdoğan regime has hounded these refugees as so-called Fetos. So, when an official government of a NATO country publicly says that this group of Turkish refugees are terrorists, this cry will strike fear into the hearts of many of the Western governments. So too will the Dutch government. Formal questions were raised in this country's government, leading to a well-known Dutch professor (Islam expert) at the University of the City of Utrecht (Prof. Dr.

Martin van Bruinesse) being commissioned by the Dutch government to launch an extensive investigation into the nature of specifically these Turkish refugees. After completing his research, his conclusion was that this group of refugees can never and will never be terrorists and that there is absolutely no threat whatsoever from these people. It turned out that these people are mainly highly educated Turks who integrate quickly and definitely do not cause any nuisance, and preferably want to earn their own living again (i.e., contribute to the Dutch economy) as soon as possible.

I am happy and grateful that freedom of opinion, press and religion is constitutionally enshrined in the Netherlands and that these Turkish people can therefore return to a normal rhythm of life here. Their resilience and positivism is truly commendable: all respect to them!

So, the fact that you don't have these freedoms in Turkey (anymore) indicates a democratic decay of unprecedented magnitude. For the sake of political and economic interests, there remains no condemnation of this behaviour and no significant pressure on this Turkish regime that now looks more like a brutal dictatorship.

The question I pose at the top of this article can now be answered: speak out on this!

**Cees Buys**
*Author and Entrepreneur*

It's an essential reference book for everyone to know that human rights are about the right to live as a human being and the right to live in dignity, equality, and freedom. These freedoms are fundamental human rights. Any attempt at tampering with these fundamental human rights is a gross violation of human rights and must be challenged at all costs!

**Adv Mohamed Shafie Ameermia**
*Former Commissioner on the South African Human Rights Commission.*

# PROLOGUE

This book is based on long-term observations, social events and what is being done to address human rights violations. It tries to be the voice of people whose rights are taken away, who are silenced and sent to prison in today's Turkey. It tries to be the cry of silenced journalists. It touches upon the stories of lost lives. It reveals important neglects regarding minorities once again. It leaves a note in history as an archive.

Book has two main parts:

1.  Conscience for Justice

2.  Unheard Stories

This book is written on behalf of millions of innocent people who are jailed and silenced in Turkey. This book is written to load a serious responsibility to ideas, words. The book let them free to fly to reach hearts of conscientious people of this era. This book is the story of innocence. This book is the story of betrayal. This book is the story of democracy, seeking for basic human rights.

Dutch artist and performer dear Nell Berger enriched the book with her illustrations. The book also features the view and opinion of MP Omer Faruk Gergerlioğlu, Former Commissioner on the South African Human Rights Commission Adv Mohamed Shafie Ameermia. Also, thanks for intro to Cees Buys, author and entrepreneur from Netherlands.

The book translation went through a local and foreign editorial board. It was brought to the printing stage after long efforts.

I have my sincere appreciation to my wife who assists and encourages me for my articles. I am very thankful to my friend Josh from London, my editor Ali Topdag from Crab Publishing, exiled journalist Bulent Kenes for his additional ideas and inspiring comments. And of course thanks to AST Advocates of Silenced Turkey. Many thanks to my friends who contributed to my book.

This book is dedicated to thousands of silenced people in Turkey between the years 2016-2023.

**M. Ertuğrul Incekul**
November 20, 2022

**Part One**

# CONSCIENCE FOR JUSTICE

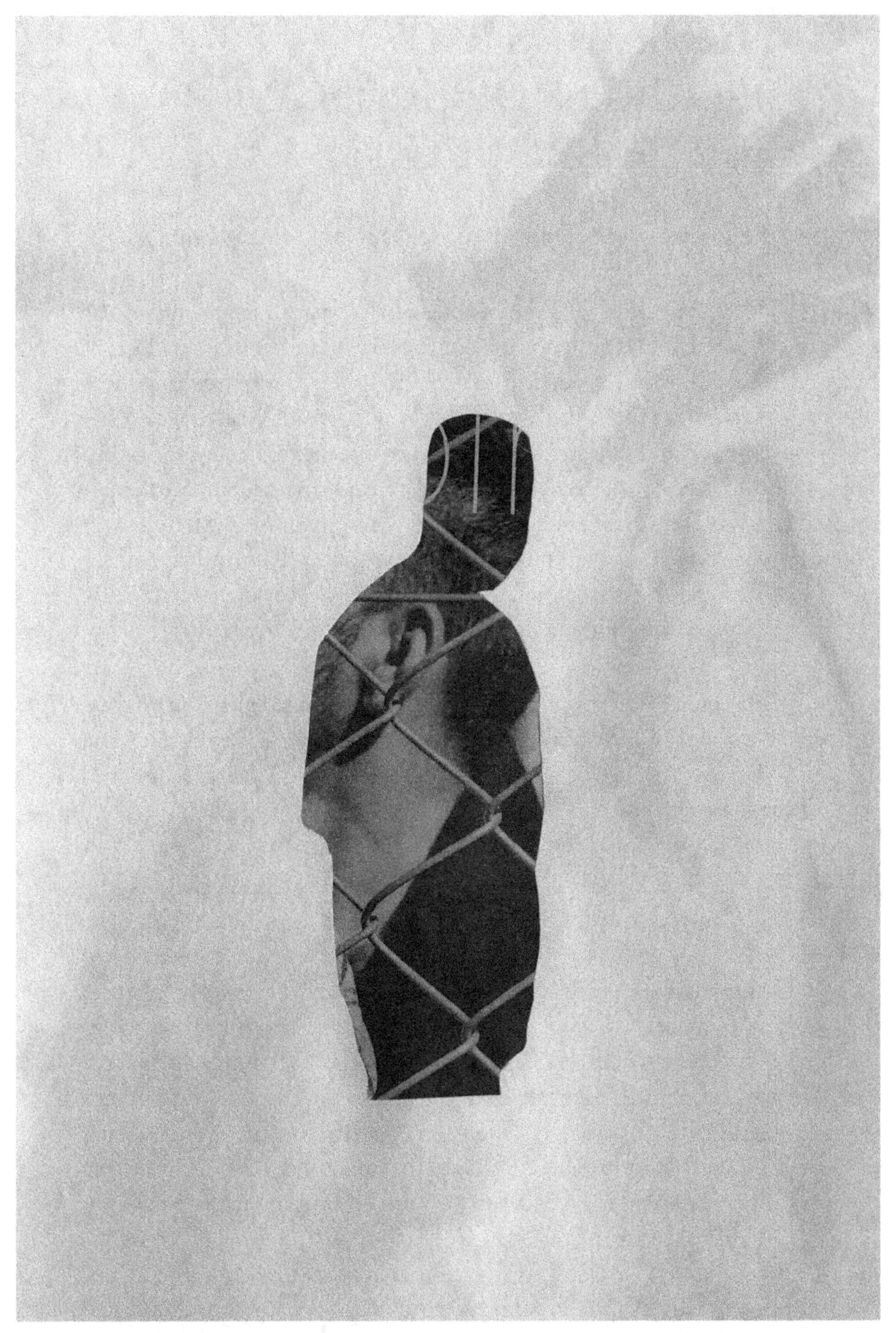

# THE SNAIL'S PACE PROGRESS OF JUSTICE IN STRASBOURG

The story of the pursuit of justice is as old as humanity.

Pierre-Henri Teitgen, one of the founding fathers of the ECHR (European Court of Human Rights), said in his famous speech to the PACE in 1949 when Europe was still recovering from the wounds of the Second World War, "No one can look many years into the future and claim their civilisation will not degenerate into totalitarianism and dictatorship and their country is free from such risks. This is why we must act first and create a consciousness and a conscience that will sound the alarm bells when the time arrives. And this special conscience can only be created through an exclusive European Supreme Court."

Ten years after this speech, the ECHR was finally established in 1959. 47 Council of Europe members recognise the jurisdiction of the European Court of Human Rights, located in Strasbourg, France.

To move the ECHR, a petitioner must first seek their rights in their home country i.e., exhaust domestic judicial remedies. Thousands of volunteers living in Europe convened in Strasbourg on Friday 24 June,2022 to raise the voices of elderly people, pregnant women, babies, and all victims and the oppressed who are subjected to human rights violations, tortured, abducted, kidnapped, and incarcerated in prisons in Turkey, where domestic rule of law is in tatters, to the ECHR (European Court of Human Rights). The event was organised by 24 civil society organisations and the Peaceful Actions Platform with the hashtag #JusticeForALLinTurkey and the slogan "Justice for All or Justice Delayed is Not Justice". With the participation of activists from different walks of life, messages of support from MPs from different countries and a concert by musician Süvari, colourful scenes were experienced.

To the ears of sadists, tyrants and dictators, the favourite music is the sigh and suffering of the oppressed. The oppressors derive pleasure from the agony of the oppressed and act harsher. What they dislike the most are the oppressed seeking their rights. Bent on oppression and destruction, dictators and their stooges go haywire when they see the motivation of the oppressed in claiming their rights. In Europe, the tortoise symbolises success through perseverance. During the event in Strasbourg, one demonstrator in a snail outfit was holding a placard with the slogan "ECHR, even I am faster than you", highlighting the snail's pace over the tortoise in slowness. Thousands called for justice with a resonant voice. Thousands seeking justice in Turkey sent messages of thanks and congratulations to the organising committee on social media.

The messages of support clearly emphasised the need for a march in quest of justice:

Costas Mavrides (Member of the European Parliament): "There is a country in our region where being a journalist is such a dangerous profession that can end you up in prison. You can find yourself behind bars for being a pro-peace academic. In this country it suffices to be Kurdish, or more simply to be a supporter of democracy and justice, to be categorically accused of being a "terrorist" or a "traitor".

There is a country in our region where hundreds of thousands of public employees stand dismissed from their jobs without a fair trial. In this country, MPs are imprisoned, mayors are dismissed and replaced by the "pawns of the regime". Also in this country, the judiciary has become an instrument to impose the political aspirations of the government. This is Turkey, a country ruled by a tyrannical regime and where people do not even have the hope of a fair trial. We cannot remain silent! Remaining silent is equal to being an accomplice to what is happening in Turkey and to all crimes against humanity!"

Canne Kanimba: "I am the daughter of Paul Rusesabagina. My father was kidnapped and tortured by the Rwandan dictatorship. He was accused of terrorism. Now he is illegitimately imprisoned, and his voice is silenced because my father fights for democracy, justice, peace, human rights, and the rule of law. He pays a price for his struggle.

Nowadays, two million people in Turkey face similar, unjust accusations of 'terrorism". This is done to silence them and prevent them from speaking out loudly for the values we all stand for together, and I stand with you."

Dietmar Köster (Member of the European Parliament): "The European Union must stand with all journalists, activists and organisations against injustice."

Andrej Hunko (Member of the Council of Europe): "Hundreds of thousands of people have been convicted under the terrorism law in Turkey in recent years. This law is like a "chewing gum", so much so you can imprison all opponents who criticise the government under this law."

Marie Arena (Chairperson of the European Parliament Human Rights Committee): "The conditions in Turkey are massively upsetting. We visited Turkey with the Human Rights Committee (DROI) and met several members of civil society, judges, lawyers, and journalists. They all told us it was immensely tough to defend human rights there. The dismissal of thousands of judges and prosecutors by the authoritarian regime in Turkey, the imprisoned journalists, and especially political prisoners and the Kavala case worry us immensely."

Legendary footballer Hakan Şükür: "I wish I could be with

you in front of the ECHR building today. I love Turkey so much, but unfortunately, I cannot go back there. I have my indelible experiences and memories there. I miss my friends so much. There is no independent judiciary in Turkey, and without it, there is nothing to protect individuals against injustice. Ten years ago, because of objecting to the human rights violations of the current regime and for taking a stand in favour of law and justice, my family and I were targeted. I was stigmatized with black propaganda. My wife's workplace was pelted with stones and my children were pestered. My work opportunities were usurped from me, false news was spread against me. Although there was no indictment or investigation against me, my entire assets were confiscated by the regime, like it did to several other people with opposing views. They put my beloved father in prison and made him suffer a great deal of torture despite his poor health. They even approached me with repulsive offers saying, "We will release your father once you return to Turkey". They even arrested my lawyer whom I had authorised for legal matters. They are afraid to even mention my name on TV channels. Hundreds of thousands of people suffer the same what I went through."

British MP Jeremy Corbyn took the stage to support the organisation and said, "Fundamental human rights must be protected wherever they are around the world. Those who challenge political tyranny must be supported."

What Balzac says, "Conscience is our unerring judge until we finally stifle it."

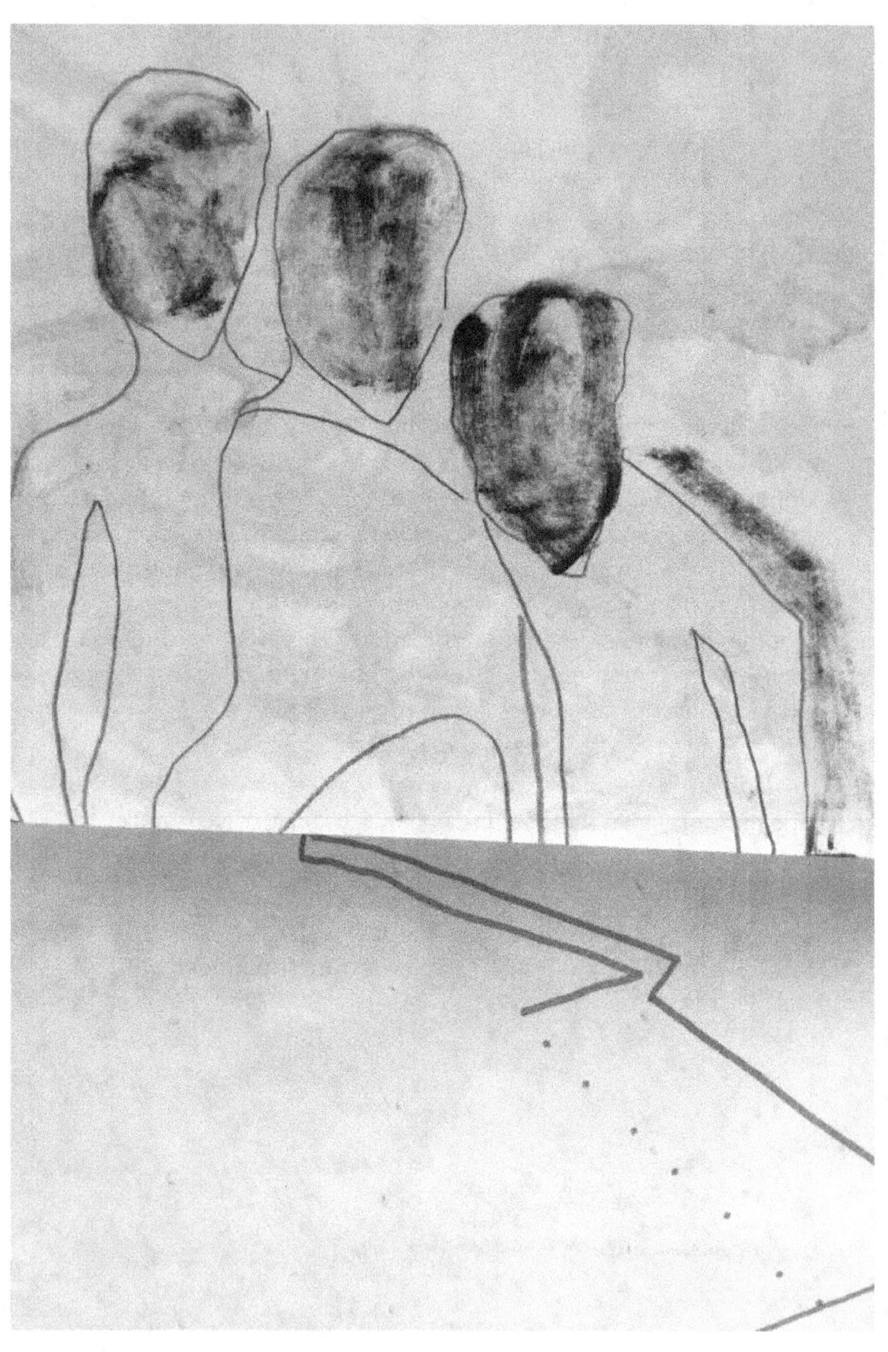

# THE BANALITY OF EVIL

The banality of evil, the subtitle of a book by the political scientist Hannah Arendt, reigns worldwide. Hannah Arendt struggles to understand the banality of evil. Arendt redefines the meaning of our most treasured political concepts and principles freedom, society, identity, truth, equality.

In Ben-Gurion's words, "We want to show all the nations of the world that the Nazis murdered millions of people simply because they were Jews and a million babies simply because they were Jewish-born babies." Or "We want the world community to recognize that Nazi Germany alone cannot be held responsible for the destruction of six million Jews of Europe. Therefore, we want the nations of the world to perceive this and be ashamed."

The AKP regime in Turkey has recently sent educator Ayşe Özdoğan, a Stage 4 cancer patient, to solitary confinement and virtually to her death. With her husband in prison, Ayşe Özdoğan's young son Burak too was left unattended. Evil should not have become this much banal. For the first time, the voice of a victim has resonated this wide across the country. Consciences should not have been so dumbed down regarding an ailing woman given a few months to live and was embraced by people from all walks of life not withstanding her identity!

These evils must be announced to the whole world, and humanity must hear this shame even after many decades. It should be our duty to make the voices of not only Ayşe's but all those who have been subjected to the sufferings and shame of this period heard and to sympathize with their cries. We are human to the extent we can sense the agony of others, regardless of their identities.

Some judges presiding over the Turkey Tribunal's trials of conscience in Geneva refused to eat after listening to the dramatic stories and torture inflicted on the defendants. They could not control their tears while listening to some defendants.

To prevent evil from becoming banal and not to surrender the world to the evil John Milton described in his book titled Paradise Lost that we must take refuge in the harbour of goodness. We must believe that goodness has abundant power to burn all evil. In societies where there are goodness and good people, there will always be hope and peace.

Actually, the struggle between good and evil is our oldest human story. In the struggle of good and evil, races, colours, and nations are already blurred and sometimes erased.

Humanity is divided into those who can embrace and appreciate humanity and existence, those who can interpret life, those who can complete the search for meaning, and others.

The tragedy of Syrian girl Nahla Osman who used to live in a camp in Idlib was very tragic. She was chained by her father. She was 6 years old. She was rescued when she was about to starve to death, but she choked to death as she quickly ate the food handed to her. The shame of the cause of her death was sufficient to be equally distributed to all humanity...

To prevent evil from becoming banal, let us first remain the good ones, and then, despite all evil, let us fly the banner of goodness in our towns.

The world is not suffering because of evil and cruel people; the world is suffering because of the good people who keep silent against the evil.

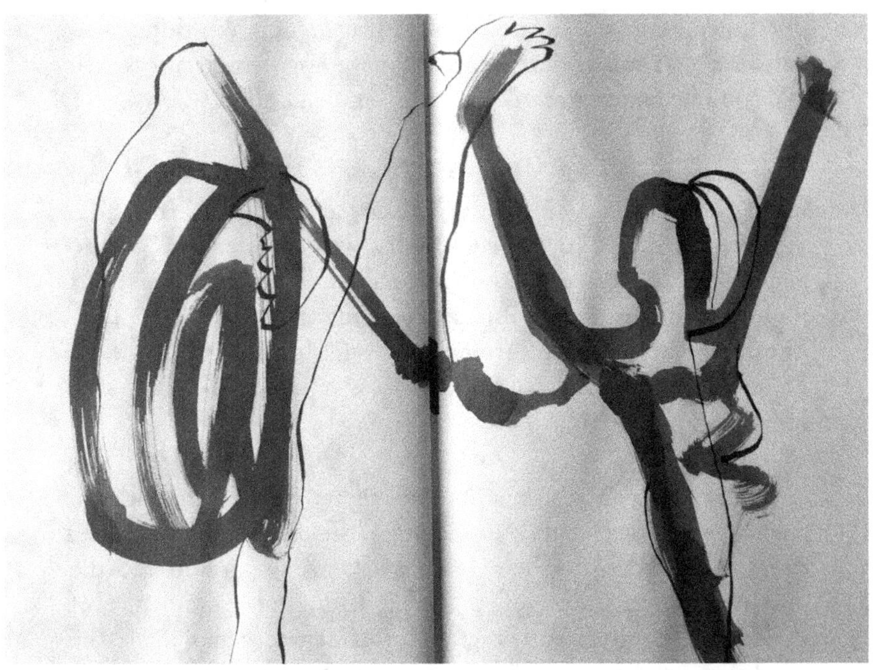

# SORRY, WE ARE ARMENIAN

Unfortunately, minority rights violations still continue in less developed democracies. Aunt Melahat was our next-door neighbour. She was so good to me when I was a child. When she was about to pass away, I found out her real name was Maria and that she was Armenian.

"I don't know if you are aware of this... We can no longer trade jokes with one another, we have become rather wary. Yet how much fun we used to have, didn't we, when we would be deep in conversation telling Turkish, Kurdish, Laz, Jewish, and Armenian jokes? We would never get hurt.

These were common products of our common culture. We would modify a Kurd into a Laz, a Jew into an Armenian, and so on, depending on the occasion. Unfortunately, our differences have been so much demonized that we are even afraid to tell jokes to one another each other... " (Hrant Dink)

In the early 1800s, Ottoman authority gaps and substantial wars led to several domestic and social problems. In 1887, the Marxist-oriented Hunchak Party was founded in Geneva, Switzerland, followed by the Dashnak Armenian organizations founded in Tbilisi, where Russian Armenians too were influential. The first clash between Armenians and Muslims broke out in Erzurum in 1890 and triggered successive incidents in Kayseri, Merzifon and Yozgat.

Hence, Armenians sought their rights in the international arena. In history, the rivalry among the Armenian fractions, the interventions of their foreign extensions in Turkey, the manipulative attitudes of the Unionists (the Committee of Union and Progress Party), and the Armenian gangs made the condition of Armenian citizens living in Ottoman territories more complicated.

Said Nursi defended his community against Armenian gangs near his village Nurs, but he returned innocent women and children back to their homes and demonstrated a clear stance back then about not harming the innocent even in war. However, at that point, there were few statements from religious authorities supporting this issue.

In 1920, some minority rights violations imposed by the Treaty of Sevres were subsequently revealed with the Treaty of Lausanne and the memories of a bygone era were erased. The rights of Armenians and other minorities and the decisions of the War Crimes Tribunals were rendered ineffective. Before the deportation, approximately 40 thousand Armenians lived in Malatya. Armenians were engaged in trade and farming in Malatya and had three large churches and three high schools.

On April 24, 1915, Armenians living in Malatya, as elsewhere, were deported to Syria and Yerevan in caravans for the execution of the Deportation Law. During these deportations, they were subjected to physical and sexual abuses. Massacres ensued.

Actually, these deportations and massacres were an escape from facing our past. It also indicated the weakening of our foreign policy in the international arena, as the issue could not be resolved through diplomacy. Yet, truths have the habit of being revealed one day.

Who knows how much guilt we have in the silence of Agop from Arapkir, who had lost his immediate relatives in 1915 and pressed his pain and agony on his bosom as if they were embers, until he was stricken with cancer in 1992!

Narrating his grandchildren about all those incidents with fear still, Agop would leave a note in history.

My friend and I invited the headmistress of the Armenian School in Moscow to Turkey in the early 2000s. Even though she knew and liked us much, she did not want to attend our invitation for a long time. Finally, she could not resist the insistence and consented for visiting our country. It was an exquisite tour. We were guested in our friends' homes and had heartfelt interactions. The delegation visited the Armenian School in Istanbul and met with the school principal. They also visited the Orthodox Church. At the airport after a pleasant tour, the headmistress admitted: "I used to love you and now I love you more. I knew there were two Turkeys. For years, I took my students to the Turkish Embassy in Moscow every April 24th to protest and to defend the rights of Armenians who had been killed. My friends had discouraged me by saying 'Do not visit Turkey! They will cut you down there!' This was why I had deferred accepting your invitation for a long time. Now I see you are not different from us."

No matter what, it is always wrong to define and judge nations or social groups with stereotypes. The tyrannical aspect of the state has always existed. Using innocence for politics is one more murder.

Armenian poet Tumanyan says: "Aprek, yerekhek, bayts mez bes chabrek [Live children, but do not live like we did]".

Gilbert Bacilio:
'Excuses, daar doet de
regering ook al zo
moeilijk over.'

abortuslobby ,
zijn opzoek gegaan
en in de politiek."
chten anti-abortus-
vlucht bij conserva-
partijen, zoals in Nederlan
e en de SGP, legt Datta uit.
visten kunnen ook tot op
ken doen met centrum-
n kunnen behulpzaa
en van wetgeving.'
ristendemocraten e
rtus van twaalf weke
en geblokkeerd."
entrumrechts is niet heel happig
nperken van bestaande wetgeving.
ar zijn ze prudent in. Ze voelen aan dat
e publieke opinie dat niet zal pikken." De
nti-abortusbeweging, ziet Datta, richt zich
daarom meer en meer op rechtse flankpar
ijen. "In Duitsland is dat Alternative für
eutschland, in Frankrijk Marion Maréchal,
het nichtje van Marine Le Pen."

# BURNING BOOKS

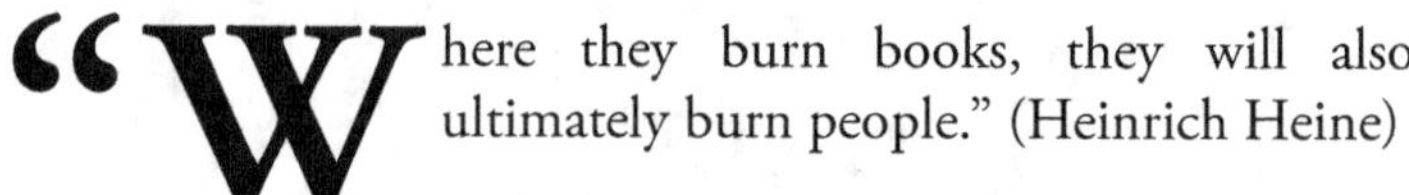

"Where they burn books, they will also ultimately burn people." (Heinrich Heine)

By burning books, the Nazis desired to get mentally and psychologically rid of the past, human knowledge, virtue and ideas. The outcome is a colossal chagrin. But in history Ibn Rushd (Averroes) was not upset when they burned his books. He explained the reason thus: "Ideas have wings, they flew, you cannot burn them either!"

One word that best describes the regime in Turkey for this period is 'insanity'. The insanity regime of AKP committed all kinds of atrocities that occurred throughout history. It did justice to insanity and delirium. It threw elderly people with Alzheimer and pregnant women into prisons. It convicted women who distributed scholarships to students or organized charity bazaars. It considered providing a grave to a victimized teacher too much for him. It plundered schools and shuttered hospitals. It managed to lock history's highest number of academics in prisons. It closed cadet colleges and sentenced cadets to life imprisonment. It proscribed public officials holding outstanding service awards as terrorists. It criminalized 1 US dollar bills and the logos of private teaching institutions printed on giveaway pens. It imprisoned a citizen working at NASA, perceiving him as an enemy of science and an element of threat. It deemed it too much for the Saturday Mothers mourning the disappeared children while seeking their rights. The list of insanity goes on and on...

No one can stop globalism and globalization anymore. News of the incidents in the remotest parts of the world spread as fast as village gossip. You cannot prevent people from accessing information with bans. The world is as close to you as the phone in your hand.

The state of insanity is a pathological condition. Delusion, on the other hand, is a manifestation of paranoia and the act of committing crimes and wreaking havoc in a state of insanity. It is the effort to implement the unsubstantiated dreams, fears, and fantasies you create in your minds, as if they were real. You declare an enemy in your imagination and try to shape life through that metaphor.

These days, dictatorial efforts to establish your own world in a state of insanity through oppression and violence rapidly diminish and become impossible worldwide. A historical example of this state of insanity is the Qarmatis.

Qarmatianism is a heretical clandestine sect founded by Hamdan ibn al-Qarmat in the ninth century AD. Hamdan was particularly influential in Iraq and its environs with his ideas of "common property" and sharing the wealth of the rich by taking advantage of the poverty of the people. The Qarmatians, pious in appearance, in reality had financial considerations, political expectations and goals. They attempted to revolt against the Abbasid caliph with the marauders they assembled, persecuted the Ahl al-Sunnah Muslims for years and martyred many. They blocked the pilgrimage routes, attacked Mecca, stole the Hajar al-Aswad (The Black Stone), and smuggled it from the Kaaba to Basra. The Qarmatians, who denied the institution of marriage, called the illicit acts (haram) as "fine arts", established partnership on disposal of women, seduced especially young people through prostitution and myriad immorality, and considered wine and similar intoxicating drinks as licit (halal). In short, the Qarmatians devised a religion according to their own whims and fancies, considered those who were not like them to be "worthy of Hellfire", and wreaked sedition and mischief for years. They may also be termed the anarchists and nihilists of their era.

So are the Kharijites. When anarchist characters are included in such groups of insanity and delirium, a complete state of madness and insanity comes into being. Here, the attitudes of the gullible people who consent to and support this condition are problematic and accountable as much as those who go insane and commit crimes. We can also call this collective and total evil an action of insanity.

Reading denotes a prominent social standing. Writing is a social responsibility one step further. Books and libraries are the memory of a society. Erasing and destroying this memory is the vision of all dictators and tyrants in a state of insanity, and this is what happened in the current period.

The most books in the history of the Republic of Turkey were burned and destroyed during this period. The savagery and horror of book burning witnessed in history during the Mongol invasion of Baghdad, the Spanish invasion of Mexico, the Nazi period in Germany, the looting of Sarajevo was regrettably experienced in the 21st century Turkey.

People dumped sacks of books into the sea, burned them in furnaces, stuffed them in bathtubs and turned them into pulp, and buried them in forests. Looting bookstores and attacking books with rage are also the tantrums of the current period...

The first quarter century of the 21st century has taken its place in history as a dark period during which books – symbols of civilization, the memory of society, the sine qua non of progress and civilization, and the mind and dreams of society – were burned and destroyed. This is a dark period in which the wretched burned an entire society and its experience just because they marginalized it and could not tolerate multivocality.

Yet, history tells us that those who burn books always lose ultimately.

ten?

# THE JURY OF CONSCIENCE

**D**on't worry! There are always judges of conscience. "Silence is indeed the most fundamental enemy of human rights. This court has singled-out this essential principle and aimed to overcome this silence." (Presiding Judge of the Turkey Tribunal Prof. Em. Dr. Françoise Baroness Tulkens).

It was not the first attempt to establish opinion courts and seek rights in other countries. The International War Crimes Tribunal, often called the Russell Tribunal, was established as presided by the British philosopher Bertrand Russell to investigate and publicize to the world the war crimes committed by the United States in Vietnam. The Tribunal was established in 1966 and its sessions were held in Stockholm and Copenhagen in 1967. Formed of representatives from 18 countries, the Russell Tribunal attracted great international attention and resonated.

However, perceived as a prejudiced and superficial organization, it was attempted to be ignored by the United States.

The World Tribunal on Iraq (WTI) is a worldwide initiative organized by the anti-war movement after the US invasion of Iraq in 2003, inspired by the Russell Tribunal for the Vietnam War. The initiative, which aims to reveal the truth about the war and occupation and to prevent the occupation from being forgotten in silence by recording the crimes and violations committed, besides the suffering, silenced voices, and resistance, envisages listening, reflection, evaluation and judgment based on concrete evidence.

In 1988, the "International Tribunal against the September 12 military regime in Turkey" was held in Cologne, Germany.

Among several issues, torture was heard as the most significant matter and witnesses were listened.

The mission of the Turkey Tribunal is to assess and report in an independent and professional manner, based on the standards and principles elaborated by other international courts and tribunals and drawing on the experience of the best practices of national courts, all allegations of human rights violations taking place under the jurisdiction of Turkish authorities.

On September 24, 2021, in Geneva, the Turkey Tribunal, constituted by former ECtHR judges and world-renowned judges, jurists and rapporteurs, ruled that Erdoğan and the AKP regime had committed systematic and organized torture and crimes that fall under the category of 'crimes against humanity'.

Geneva-based tribunal 'Turkey Tribunal' heard witnesses on torture and rights violations in Turkey. After five days of symbolic trials, the verdict is published: "Cases can be transferred to The Hague."

Maria Arena, Chair of the European Parliament's Sub-Commission on Human Rights, attended the Turkey Tribunal as an observer and expressed her regret: "The testimonies of victims of human rights violations are deeply moving, and the lack of trust in the Turkish judicial system is an important reason for these testimonies."

Meltem Oktay: "I was in Nusaybin for six months and reported on all incidents to publicize them. I was made a target. There were several foreign reporters and journalists, and most of them were detained."

Mehmet Alp: "Handcuffed behind my back and with a sack over my head, I was taken to a place in Şanlıurfa, handed over to the MIT (National Intelligence Organization) and beaten. I was tortured for 24 days."

Lawyer Eren Keskin: "I have never even held a gun. I have always been in favour of peaceful solutions. Yet, currently, I have been labelled as a member of an armed organization. Torture has been a state policy in Turkey for years."

Prof. Dr. Flückiger Yves: "Human rights are for everyone. No one can be deprived of this right in any way."

Eric Sottas: "Torture is unacceptable under any circumstances. Those who commit torture must be sentenced to at least several years in prison."

The Tribunal heard the testimonies of Mehmet Alp, Erhan Doğan and Eren Keskin on torture. Mustafa Özben, Mesut Kaçmaz and Gökhan Güneş's lawyer Sezin Uçar were heard on abduction. Meltem Oktay and Cevheri Güven testified on violations of press and freedom of expression. On impunity, Tülay Açıkkollu (wife of Gökhan Açıkkollu), Ercan Kurkut (brother of Kemal Kurkut), and Barbaros Şansal testified.

Faysal Sarıyıldız, Hasan Dursun and Süleyman Bozoğlu testified on access to justice and judicial independence.

The Turkey Tribunal includes these experienced specialists:

Presiding Judge Prof. Em. Dr. Françoise Baroness Tulkens; Former Judge and Vice President of the European Court of Human Rights Dr. Johann van der Westhuizen, Former Judge of the Constitutional Court of South Africa

Angelita Baeyens; Robert F. Kennedy Vice President for International Advocacy and Litigation for Human Rights and Adjunct Professor of Law at Georgetown University Law Center Prof. Em. Dr. Giorgio Malinverni; Vice President of the Administrative Court of the Council of Europe Prof. Dr. Ledi Bianku; Associate Professor at the Faculty of Law and Institute of

Political Sciences of the University of Strasbourg and European Human Rights Judge Dr. John Pace; Former Secretary-General of the United Nations Commission on Human Rights.

Here are the conclusions of the court's closing day report:

"The Tribunal found that the Government of Turkey failed to comply with international conventions on torture."

"The Tribunal found the Government of Turkey guilty of 'forced abductions'. It was clear that the Government of Turkey had engaged in forced abductions and forced disappearances."

"The Tribunal clearly observed a state-led crackdown on freedom of the press and freedom of expression in Turkey."

"Politicians have stern influence on the judiciary in Turkey. The Turkish government does not fulfil its international obligations on press freedom."

"Forced abductions take place at home and abroad through the MIT (National Intelligence Organization) and the Turkish government acknowledges this. Abductions take place in Turkey in broad daylight, in clear view of cameras and witnesses."

"The dismissal of 4560 judges and prosecutors through a list profiled by the HSYK (Supreme Council of Judges and Prosecutors) denotes the intimidation and intimidation of the judiciary."

"If the testimonies and reports presented during the Tribunal are brought to the attention of international judicial authorities, all these crimes will be categorized as 'crimes against humanity' and the accused can face severe penalties."

(For detailed information, please visit https://turkeytribunal. com/tr/karar/)

Bertrand Russell summarises the main task:

"We are not judges. We are witnesses. Our task is to make mankind bear witness to these horrible crimes and to unite humanity on the side of justice in Vietnam."

# IT'S NOT ONLY
# AN ELECTION

**In** developed countries, elections are not an extraordinary event for citizens. It is discussed for a few weeks, posters are put up, news and comments are made, and people go about their business and daily life eventually. Yet is it the same in countries like Turkey? Those who observe Turkey may think it is virtually the Judgement Day. Why? Because elections and leaders may touch our lives in such a way, they affect our lives in all aspects.

In countries like Turkey, where democracy, law, and human rights are not deep-seated, what the "holy state", the supreme chiefs, and the elected mighty leaders decide and think about the citizens is more important than what the citizens think.

This is precisely the situation in the Eastern societies, where people who have no doubt about the righteousness of Prophet Moses, despite knowing all the evil, crimes, and wrongdoings of Pharaoh, are slaves to the pathetic idea "he gives us our bread". It must be the consequence of this despicable frame of thought that the proponents of leftist or rightist political views stay mum even when human rights violations smell to high heaven. It must be for this reason that those who never shut up for their religious sensitivities feign the silence of lambs about the atrocities suffered by their neighbours next door.

It's not many public figures who have stood up for the oppressed notwithstanding whether they belonged to the same community with them, who have not questioned the affiliation of the oppressed, who have not remained silent about all the human rights violations, persecutions and tortures committed under the Erdoğan regime. There have been academics, politicians, bureaucrats, journalists from democratic countries worldwide, especially from Europe and America, who have reacted to the illegitimate acts.

From Turkey, the first individuals who come to my mind without straining my memory are Ömer Faruk Gergerlioğlu, Enes Kanter, Hüda Kaya, Kazım Güleçyüz, Züleyha Gülüm, Sezgin Tanrıkulu, Ahmet Altan, Cemre Birand, Natali Avazyan, Zülfü Livaneli, Ahmet Nesin, Şebnem Korur Fincancı, Eren Keskin.

The 'disinformation' bill, now known as the Censorship Law, was passed by the Turkish Parliament. Social media still sets the agenda in Turkey. What is wanted to be accomplished nowadays is to put the last nail in the coffin. The charge of "disseminating misleading information to the public", a notion with no legal equivalent, envisages a prison sentence of one to three years for those who allegedly engage in disinformation. Not only journalists, but also common people, politicians and civil society organizations will be victimized by this law.

It is futile to expect elected leaders to save the country unless the law and the judiciary are independent, and the constitution is secured. It is essential to discern differences and not to paint the world in the same colour. Anything else is dictatorship and autocracy. It is a betrayal of science, morality, wisdom, tradition and, above all, humans.

# LIVING IN HIDING AND TRAUMAS

"Sick people are the products of a sick culture. Healthy people can flourish in a healthy culture only." (Maslow)

Living in hiding is traumatic. People are afraid of AKP regime in Turkey. They prefer living in hiding. Traumatic situations are inevitable in groups that are silenced, subjected to violence and oppression, or in children exposed to family violence. I would like to leave the psychological dimension of this issue to the experts and share important points about its sociological and social dimension.

What happened in the past to the Kurds, Armenians, Alevis or the emigrant community from Salonica in Turkey and what happens to the Hizmet Movement nowadays are examples of mass traumatic situations. What happened to the Roma, Blacks and Jews worldwide are also included in these. Such minorities are demonized through perception operations. They are dehumanized and devalued as non- human beings. They are showcased as entities that have no value in the eyes of society and should not even be considered as humans. They are portrayed as the prime enemy of the country and society, and the main culprit and perpetrator of all the evils and crimes of the past and the present. As known, this was precisely the perception management carried out under the intellectual leadership of Goebbels during the Holocaust, and over time, lies and perceptions grew into the state policy. The people subjected such violence and oppression are alienated or forced to alienate from their relations and attachments over time.

The question that needs to be appraised here is: Such mass exterminations, annihilations or genocides have always happened, as the human history has witnessed the calamities inflicted by several barbarians and despotic leaders with blood on their hands, which are the disgrace of humanity. Yet, what kind of a stance can we, who are subjected to these atrocities and oppressed by the ruthless, take? Is this in our hands?

Life is a tangle of choices. The way of looking at life, the viewpoint, and the perspective determine the colour and tone of life. Sometimes people have no strength to resist the events, and they let it be, saying, "I am tired of life".

However, the Creator does not leave us to ourselves. We are always nudged with tidings of sunshine and spring. We receive the urge in our hearts and minds to hold on to life again, and to start everything again. And it is up to us to notice that glare and that warning message to hold on to life again, and to be on the path of goodness and conscience once more. Despite those who attempt to darken our lives, we need the effort to turn towards the One Who bestows life. The choice is ours; we will either be among the good or the bad. If people lose their sense of compassion and mercy, there is nothing left of their humanity.

Severe pressures and fear lead to secrecy. Examples to these include state pressure, pressure within people's own communities, peer pressure, and family pressure. If they are less affected by social pressure after some stage, secrecy becomes a choice; people may prefer to use nicknames or initials rather than their full names in such periods of fear.

Living in secrecy can lead to a contradiction with one's past, an inability to integrate into one's society, a feeling of being a loser, and a lack of self-confidence in one's surroundings. Not being able to attend the meetings, conversations, and activities that one used to do regularly, having to hide one's affiliation, not being able to express one's values, beliefs and culture have negative and traumatic consequences both for oneself and one's family members.

Millions of people have been forced to live under such conditions in Turkey and the traumas experienced by those subjected to such a regime of fear and violence have been inevitable. The crime and responsibility of the regime which placed people under these conditions are massive. Yet, despite everything, all these hardships can be overcome through a fiction like done by Guido in the movie "Life is Beautiful", who struggles to alleviate the bitter realities of war by venturing to make his son see the war, the prisoners in the concentration camps and everything as a game, by telling him that if he becomes a good boy, he will buy him the toy tank he has wanted so much. The elixir of willpower bestowed by the Creator upon humans holds the power of overcoming hardships far beyond imagination, provided they do not squander their willpower or exhaust it pointlessly, and they do not fall into the abyss of despair.

In a social sense, the Hizmet Movement was present and contributed to several key disciplines in Turkey. With thousands of schools, thousands of dormitories, thousands of university exam prep and tutoring centres, dozens of universities, dozens of hospitals, newspapers, TV channels, magazines, Abant Meetings, and humanitarian relief and charitable assistance through the Kimse Yok Mu Solidarity and Aid Association in times of need, it significantly contributed to Turkey and its citizens in the fields of education, culture, finance, health and media. Intellectuals from all walks of life expressed these several times, even though they cannot say so nowadays out of fear.

Hizmet, with its presence in 170 countries worldwide, has carried out activities in the fields of education, culture and finance, appreciated by the local authorities depending on the economic and democratic standards of the countries where the institutions are located, and still continues its successful work globally excluding a few anti-democratic countries. Myriad tests and problems awaited the Hizmet Movement people who had to migrate abroad, especially those who sought asylum in democratic countries like the European Union, United States of America, and Canada. They braced tests and challenges in brand new areas such as learning a foreign language, adapting to a new culture and a different environment, being subjected to an altogether different bureaucracy, holding on to life on their own, and adapting to new education styles. I think notwithstanding all appalling events that has taken place during the six years since July 15, 2016, coup attempt, we have come a long way in terms of survival, resuming life and integrating to our host countries. I receive heartening news from friends and colleagues in many countries. I hear about several friends holding on to life, adapting their children to the schools in their respective countries, starting their own businesses, learning the local language, making new friends, and I feel immensely happy. I had tackled this issue in my article titled "Stories of the New Europeans". I believe we will receive more good news in years to come.

Now, let's again ask the question we asked at the beginning: What kind of a stance will we take in response to the ruthless folk who upset our lives just for their gains and despicable interests? Will we alter our human values, ideals, and path for which we have paid a great price and whose truth is beyond doubt? Will we disloyally ignore our past? Or will we lend an ear to our conscience, take common sense as a guide, and continue to struggle against the authoritarian mindset that ignores and persecutes us for the truths and universal values we rationally believe through common sense?

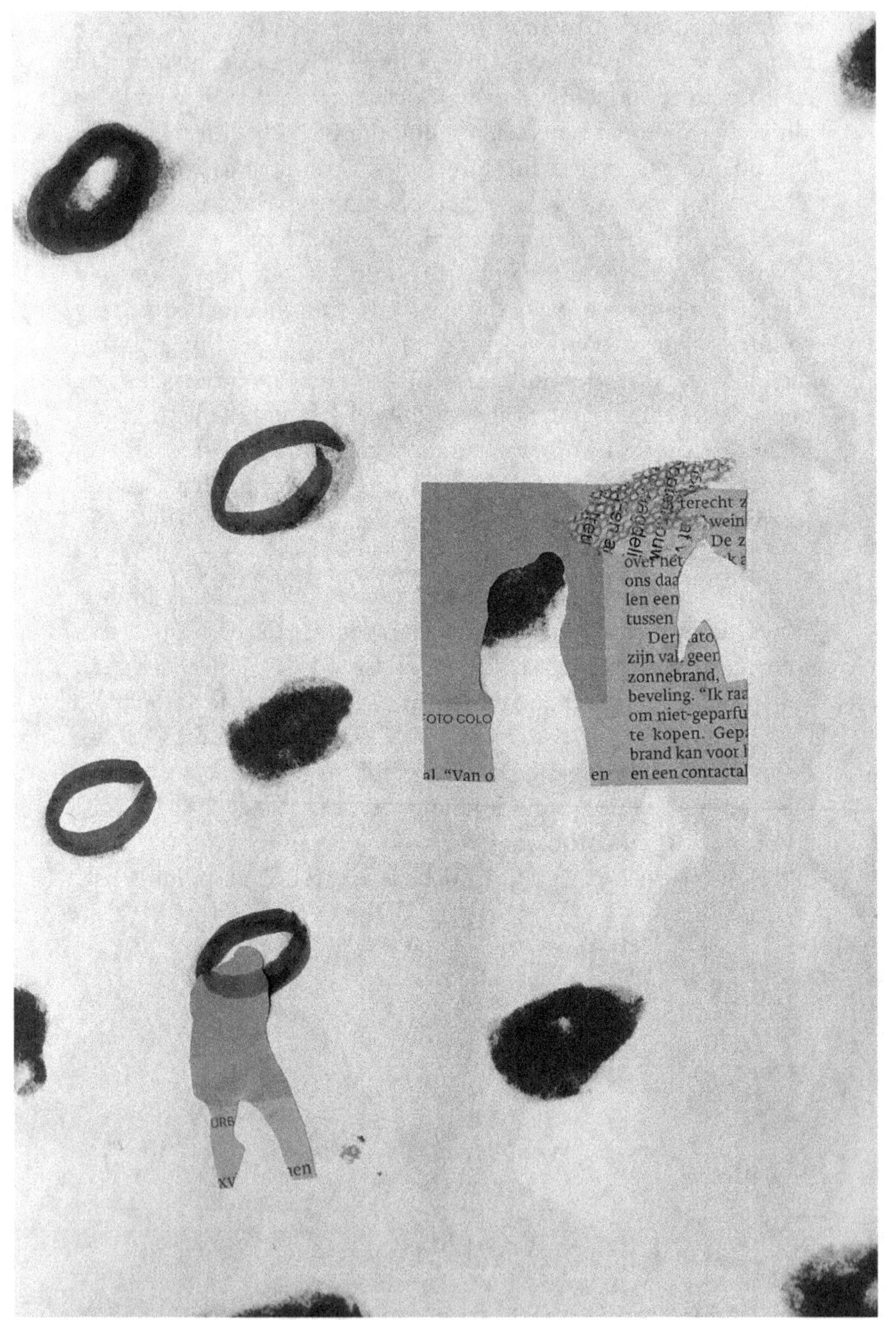
terecht z
wein
De z
over het
ons daa
len een
tussen
Der ato
zijn val geen
zonnebrand,
beveling. "Ik raa
om niet-geparfu
te kopen. Gep
brand kan voor
OTO COLO
al. "Van o
en    en een contactal

# PARADIGMS, OUR INTELLIGENTSIA AND SILIVRI

Şahin Alpay is an intellectual whom I have been following and drawing inspiration from for years. His article "My New Worldview" impressed me a lot. I read with sadness how our true intellectuals were pushed into isolation by the human rights violations, lawlessness, arbitrariness, and a despotic regime distancing from democracy. If these people lived in a democratic country, they would be the top-grade minds cherished and retained as university professors with high salaries, and work as consultants and columnists.

"As one lives, one realizes that everything changes over time, and what seemed true yesterday may seem different today" says Şahin Alpay. It will be the same tomorrow; whom they dub terrorists today, they will laud as heroes tomorrow. The same as they restored dignity to people who had once been witch-hunted. What is the use, though? Poet Nazım Hikmet died with homesickness and reproach. Poet and activist Mehmet Akif Ersoy spent his most productive years in exile in Egypt. Mandela lived in prison on Robben Island for 28 years.

The fundamental element in liberalism is the individual. Peoples, communities, and nations are all composed of individuals and individuals shape history. Like leftist intellectual Ahmet Altan or conservative intellectual Ali Ünal meet today on the same axis of victimization and shape history... Like HDP MP Ömer Faruk Gergerlioğlu defending mother of a Cadet, Melek Çetinkaya. In true liberalism, the individual is fundamental. Idea, belonging, nationality is not the main theme.

We have clearly observed how many so-called intellectuals are indeed cowards, servants and slaves to power and wealth.

Şahin Alpay says "Yes, one cannot live without believing in a cause (discovering something, inventing something, realizing something, loving something/a person, etc.)" in his article. True! It is meaningless to live without faith, ideals, dreams etc. However, fights involving political interests are futile and fleeting.

Journalist Yavuz Baydar recently said in an interview from France that it is hard to remain an independent journalist in Turkey where we have a culture of tribalism and subservience. Yes, democracy is a luxury in eastern societies like Turkey. African societies are the same, they pluck the fruit if it is too ripe. Hasn't the state been devouring its own children for years? It has never been satiated. For this reason, the majority of Turkish intellectuals are abroad; Turkey has been suffering brain drain for years. Over time, a strong Turkish intellectual diaspora will emerge in democratic countries abroad.

Let's change it a bit and conclude this article for our people and intellectuals who are paying the price in Silivri: If everyone says what they think, if everyone makes an effort in this regard, we can attain a beautiful future together with our common effort.

# CAMÕES AND
# COLONIAL HISTORY

Colonialism is the shameless face of civilization.

In the second half of the 18th century, two thinkers, Baron de Montesquieu, a Frenchman, and Jeremy Bentham, a British, argued that trade was a check on the barbarian sentiment embodied in war. Luís Vaz de Camões (b. 1524 - d. June 10, 1580) was a Portuguese poet. He was born in Lisbon. He was the son of Simão Vaz de Camões and Ana de Sá e Macedo, and a scion of the high Portuguese nobility of the Vimioso and Da dynasty. An inspiration for European poets and epics. Master of lyric poetry. Compared to the likes of Homer and Dante... His influence is conceivably wider.

His work Os Lusiadas transcends the centuries. A poet of lyrical poems that reflect the spirit of Portugal's maritime expeditions and conquests. He tells the story of Vasco da Gama's discovery of the sea route to the Indies. He rewrites history with his epics. Meanwhile, the Luís Vaz Collection is lost. He was a good geographer and a man of letters. He was also a soldier. Part of his life was spent on sea voyages. Sometimes he barely escaped with his life. A sophisticated poet he was. One who laid the groundwork for the Renaissance much earlier. He spends 17 years on unrecorded Indian adventures. He did not make a fortune there, as he often complained in his poetry about his bad luck and the injustices he faced. While in the East, he participated in a few naval expeditions and, as he alludes to in his epic, was shipwrecked in the Mekong Delta. It can be assumed that his years in the East were similar to those of thousands of Portuguese scattered at that time from Africa to Japan; as he says, he did not make a fortune in life. Luís de Camões died in absolute poverty on June 10, 1580, in Lisbon, Portugal. According to some biographers, Camões did not even have a sheet to be used as a shroud. He was buried in a shallow grave. Later, in 1594, Dom Gonçalo Coutinho commissioned a tombstone for him engraved with the words: "Here lies Luís de Camões, the Prince of Poets of his time. He lived poor and so died."

Many countries have colonial histories. They all have a history of exploitation and human rights violations. While they differed in outreach, they all have a history of taking over free countries through oppression, and of siphoning off the wealth of those countries. Unfortunately, it is an undeniable fact that even within their own country, they suppress minorities they perceive as a threat with bloodshed, try to destroy them and use state terror.

British historian Eric Hobsbawn uses the concept of the "Long 19th century", which began with the French Revolution in 1789 and ended with the outbreak of World War I in 1914. Within the frame of this concept, the 20th century, which began in 1915, will probably enter a new era with the attack on Ukraine in 2022. Nowadays, we are witnessing Russia's invasion of Ukraine. Ukraine is a country where people have always been suppressed for years and have never been allowed to develop. Its people have always suffered and continue to suffer. Putin has finally ignored the West and the United States and declared war on the Zelensky government, whose pro-American administration he has long been uncomfortable with.

Putin's name will undoubtedly take a prominent place in colonial history. More recently, Russia took advantage of Turkey's strategic vacuum to intervene in Georgia, Azerbaijan, Syria, Crimea, Kazakhstan, and other countries, and etched its name firmly in the annals of tyranny. The West started with the usual condemnations, but then removed Russia from the EU Security Council. It also suspended the 10-odd billion-euro worth Nord Stream-2 system, provided arms to Ukraine, and invested 100 billion euros in the EU armed forces. The crisis has also been a lesson for countries like France, Italy, and Austria, which depend on Russia for their gas supplies. With the construction of two LNG terminals and the commitment to create strategic energy reserves, countries such as the Czech Republic and France have been given the green light and alternative energy production options have been made available. The US is providing Ukraine with $350 million in arms and defence aid. NATO member states have closed their airspace to Russia. The most severe financial sanction was undoubtedly the exclusion of some Russian financial institutions from the SWIFT network. Oligarchs lined up to withdraw their money from the Russian banks.

Nothing will ever be the same again. A war on the edge of Europe and hundreds of civilians dying... And the Ukrainian leader Zelensky, who bravely defended his country and won the sympathy and support of the world public opinion with his videos, broke the illusion. The cry of the citizens "This is Putin's war, not Russia's" and "I am Russian, and I am very sorry for what happened" exclaimed the ugly face of the war.

Nationalist Kemalists and political Islamists in Turkey who admire Russia and China may be happy with Turkey's shifting axis, but a Turkey moving away from the West promises no peace and no future to anyone. While leftists in the West severely criticize Russia, some of the Left in Turkey still try to justify Russian aggression.

Europe has learned the bitter lesson over its dependency on Russia for energy and China for raw materials, but that it should tap new sources and routes. The history of colonialism has never given peace to anyone and never will... The famous anti-war Nobel laureate Bertrand Russell's words are as valid today as they were said: "If a third world war breaks out, the loser will slip into the grave and the winner to a coma." Let's see, the world is expectant of new developments.

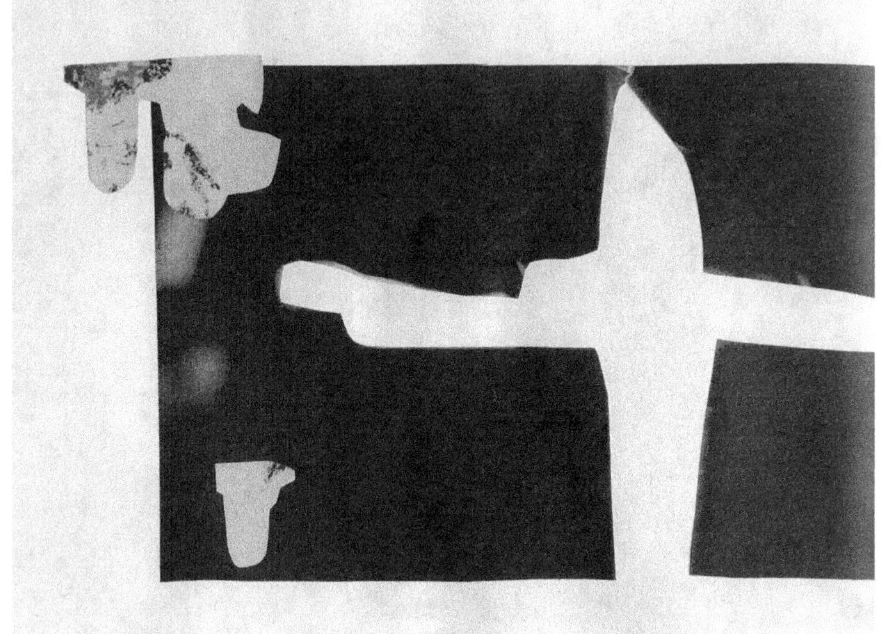

# TURKEY'S JOURNEY OF NON-DEMOCRATIZATION

**T**ime is the best interpreter. We have resembled the concepts to ourselves; we have filled them as it suits us. Even in this era, when the information technologies change the whole system of life, there are Jacobin Kemalist formations which turned their backs on the founding values of Mustafa Kemal Atatürk over time, alienated from their own culture, act as enemies of religion and defend aggressive political elitism and authoritarianism. Nationalist -isms that shifted to racism and highly capitalist political -isms which exist only for themselves and think they are to be absolved of their entire crimes by basing them on the absolute tenets of the religion, and which hollowed the moral criteria.

AK Partyism and the so-called libertarian leftist -isms, which watch the victimization of other social groups, do not bring happiness, peace, and solutions to people anymore. On the contrary, they bring forth an understanding that is more introverted, more aggressive, and more adopting the discourse of hate.

The Ottoman Empire started to follow Europe from the 1856 Reform Edict onwards. The conditions of the Treaty of Paris included the accession of this edict. The Treaty of Paris was a turning point. Those were the years when we turned our faces towards Europe and started to grant certain privileges. The difference in religions yielded a political transformation, alienating Muslims from the Christian citizens and making Europe look like a threat to their identity and political freedom. Sultan Abdul Hamid II's authoritarianism brought members of the Naqshbandi Sufi order closer to the Committee of Union and Progress in power. The members of this Sufi order forged close relations with the bureaucracy and a secular understanding of conservatism emerged. As interpreted by Prof. Dr. Kemal Karpat, to spread nationalist ideas and finally transform the Ottoman Empire into a Turkish state, the Türk Yurdu (Turkish Homestead) magazine was first published in 1911 and the Türk Ocakları (Turkish Hearths) association was founded in 1912. (The Türk Ocakları was replaced by Halkevleri (People's Houses) in 1930-31 but was reopened under the original name in 1949 as a special association to spread a new brand of nationalism).

The nationalists were opposed to the Islamists and the Westernists, with whom they differed on religion and Ottomanism issues, besides the counter-nationalist and humanist movements represented by the poet Tevfik Fikret. Nevertheless, nationalism was not officially discarded and Ottomanism continued to be the ideology of the state. With the influence of the policies of the Committee of Union and Progress to open up to the West, intellectuals like Mehmet Akif Ersoy, Necip Fazıl Kısakürek, Nurettin Topçu, Ziya Gökalp emerged with a synthesis of modernism, Islam and nationalism.

Milli Nizam Partisi (National Order Party) was founded in the beginning of the 1970s. Its political line continued with the Refah Partisi (Welfare Party) and other Islamist parties.

However, the factors that diminished the influence of the Welfare Party and paved the way for the incumbent AKP (Justice and Development Party) can be listed as the decline in the influence of political Islam worldwide, examples like Iran and Afghanistan, the secularization of ummatism, antagonism to global capital, the phase after the February 28, 1997 'post-modern coup', the discovery of Erbakan's life of luxury by those who once attributed messianic qualities to him, and their conflicts with the military.

The 1990s saw the synthesis of nationalism, conservativism, modernism, a period epitomized with Turgut Özal. Actually, the Anglo-Saxon model of moderate and conservative secularism had started with the Democrat Party (DP). The process of normalisation and opening up to the West and the world succeeded, but unfortunately this period did not last long after Özal's sudden death. In successive years, the AKP (Justice and Development Party) emerged with an Americanist, Islamist and modernist approach which did not clash with the Western values. Between 2002 and 2010, effective steps were taken in the fields of EU membership process, rule of law, democratization, and public development. When Turkish Government moved away from the Copenhagen Criteria and thus retreated from democracy and law, the country reached the brink of total collapse in fields from bureaucracy to morality, from economy to education, from foreign policy to sports, from urbanism to ecology, and from culture and arts to academia.

Blindly-followed-leader-oriented thinking based on symbols, vain heroism, marginalisation, enriching its own elite and fuelling anger has long outlived its utility. Kemalism denies the past and considers the end of the Ottoman Empire as a liberation from an obsolete empire, and its rap sheet includes severe problems with the Kurds. The darkest and the bloodiest page of the Kemalist period is undoubtedly the Dersim Massacre of 1937-38 and the anti-democratic coups and actions following it; the Kemalist regime bears a solemn guilt against its own people. The officials of the regime lost their anti-imperialist approach inherent at their starting point. Kemalism emerged with saviour principles. Although it did not resonate with the people as effectively as the French Revolution, it did resonate with the conservative intellectuals. For example, the principle of secularism; the Kemalists' efforts to protect secularism evolved into hostility to religion. The French style of secularism is Jacobin and rigid, disconnected from the conservative public. In addition, the regime officials' monopoly as the elite of the Republic and their juristic approach seriously offended groups of different opinions, and the Kemalist label was attached to related or unrelated opposition groups. This pushed Kemalism out of its orbit and rendered it obsolete. Had they been more inclusive and if they had not excluded conservatives to such an extent, we as the society might not have generated so much hatred, and we might have braced the current tsunamis of democracy gentler.

A few intellectuals who emerged from leftist factions and except for the likes of Toktamış Ateş, Cem Karaca and Ahmet Altan. The responsibilities of an intellectual are shaped not by worldview or colour distinction, but by taking a stand against human rights violations, righteousness in the pursuit of justice, and resistance to crime and criminals.

Among the qualities of being an intellectual are expressing themselves in a way that resonates in the society, being comprehensive through their words that look simple or easy, but difficult to imitate, having discourses and projects unique to themselves, not being ivory tower intellectuals, and their capacity to face the society and their past.

As the final analysis, Turkey must face the spiral of issues and problems including those that have been postponed since the founding of the Republic, the signing of the Treaty of Paris and the time Turkey started to compromise its own identity. The current systems can no longer carry the country or the society, they do not provide peace and stability. On the contrary, they generate chaos, hatred, violence, and misery. The clash between the East and the West must end. We need a synthesis of wisdom and knowledge.

As a result of pressure and negligence, the suicide of Enes Kara, a medical student, has shown that intolerance, family pressure, and an outburst of hatred towards a social group as a whole destroy the grounds for constructive discussion and deliberation. While the state does not properly audit its own institutions and private organizations, innocent lives are lost. The efforts of social groups to understand one another and our struggle for democracy should not turn into a war of judgments. Considering the other social groups as enemies, condemning them to poverty without trying to understand them, and indulging in extrajudicial executions will never lead us to reconciliation and social peace.

With the dream of the days when we will become a true society of law and democracy, a society open to modernization and where everyone is respectful of one another's beliefs and worldviews, a society at peace with its traditions...

# SILENCES OF DEATH

Writer Emine Eroğlu joined to the International Journalists Association (IJA) Talks based in Frankfurt. It was an exclusive tour d'horizon, indeed. She spoke about free thought and its limits, and Turkey and intellectual poverty. From this interview, I especially wished to share with you the notions of our intellectual poverty and deadly silences.

You witness people going mad overnight; the silence of the people you expect to speak out against injustice is worse than death. These silences are spiritual deaths. The sign of life is speech, words, expressions. With words and speech, people become human. There are secrets of humanity in the words we form. Those who remain silent are those who have lost the quality of being intellectuals in the face of history. There are also those who take pleasure in poisoning like snakes and those who speak to support oppression. Silences in the face of this truth are the silences of death. Intellectuals are the cream of the society. The cream's decay indicates the milk's decay.

The most significant indicator of being an intellectual is fearlessness. Not fearing death, isolation, or exile. It is about not being articulated to power. There are six levels of corruption; intellect is one level, and the last level is conscience. It is the silences of conscience. I was a publisher for years, I used to think I managed intellectual capital, but it turns out I was wrong. The greatest poverty is intellectual poverty. This intellectual accumulation was an accumulation detached from essence. I witnessed that the real intellectual accumulation effervesced in Hizmet because the participants of the Movement has not broken away from the essence. They have not grown silent in the face of oppression; they have not bowed down.

We are ready for our own Renaissance By talking about the Beloved, studying sciences, and enriching their own knowledge and wisdom, they maintained their words and direction against this information pollution. They formed sentences against oppression. This was a test! We have witnessed that people who looked bright like stars and deceived themselves as the sun, were indeed fireflies. We witnessed how great intellectuals the people standing humbly in the background were. There was a storm, a tremor. Those who could stand erect and those who collapsed have been separated from one another. The test of intellectuals is not over; there are only a few who can speak the truth and the realities and utter these in the name of justice.

Some are supposedly speaking in the name of justice, but they have turned Hizmet into the other of the other in a way that makes one think as if Hizmet does not exist. There are silences that ignore the thousands of sufferings experienced by the Hizmet Movement and us. Even consciences have become selective. There are so few people whom you may point and count. Ahmet Altan says, "Fear not!" I witnessed this process of fear in Turkey which started with the December 17/25 incidents. In this process which evolved into July 15, I observed how those so-called bright stars fell to the ground. I saw how they joined forces with power, how they calculated for small benefits, and how they took shelter behind certain excuses. This is why Turkey has not passed the test impartially. When this phase started, Fethullah Gülen Hodjaefendi underlined the intellectual poverty by citing the Dreyfus case as an example. While he made these references, intellectuals who once sided with the Hizmet and said, "Why does Hodjaefendi approach the issue this way?" and people whom we considered intellectuals, left the flank, and spoke against the Movement. Today we need to realize that we are paying the price of this intellectual poverty. What matters here is equipping oneself and intellectual experience. Hodjaefendi has an approach which I cherish greatly: "Through these phases, we are actually preparing for our own Renaissance."

The post-Karbala period was also a stormy phase. They all clung to a science, thinking religion was escaping their grasp. A brilliant development in religious sciences ensued and a Renaissance was experienced. During this period of tribulation, the participants of the Hizmet Movement had to scatter all over the world. Allah Almighty provided climes where young people could receive education and grow on the grounds of legitimacy. Arts and scientists will spring from this process. My concern is about being patient with this process. This wait should not be passive; it should be active, and it should be spent by acquiring new knowledge. We all need to educate ourselves well, we all need to be equipped. We need to do something on social media with this equipment. To be able to express ourselves without fear and in order not to be bought and sold like some in Turkey, we need to be conscious and distant in our relationships with corporeality, the world, and the authorities. Remaining free and having free relationships depend on our moderation in our relationships with corporeality and the world. We all need to assume the responsibility of being intellectuals. We need to have our set of expressions for proclaiming the truth and the realities, and for enjoining good and forbidding evil.

# THE JEWS OF TURKEY

**As** peoples of Anatolia, we are now minorities and immigrants in our host countries. For years, being a minority in Turkey has always been considered as a misdemeanour or a deficiency, and this understanding increasingly continues. What's more, a hostile minority policy has been pursued and fomented regardless of people's personal and human rights. Otherization has always existed in the hidden agenda of the state.

While there was a time in our history when our relations and integration with minorities (considering the world conditions of the time) were exemplary, for a long time now we have gone down in history with deportations, massacres, and hostile attitudes. It would be naïve to expect a different treatment from those who inflict such atrocities even on their own children.

The Sephardim, who constitute a significant majority of the Turkish Jewish community, came from Portugal and Spain in the 15th century. In the 19th century, there were two hundred thousand Jews in Turkey. Yet nowadays, due to the 1934 unrest in Thrace and other events, this number has decreased to seventeen thousand. The Jews of Turkey are divided into groups such as those who came from Eastern Europe, those who came from Portugal and Spain, and those who remained from Rome, Ashkenazim, Sephardim and Romaniotes.

There are 14.5 million Jews in the world. This is two per thousand of the world population. Meanwhile, 20% of the Nobel Prizes are awarded to Jews. 7 million live in Israel, and the rest live in America, Argentina, and Canada. Jews in Europe were subjected to antisemitism. In America, despite being among the founders of the United States of America, Jews were still subjected to certain restrictions. Jews define the period between the reigns of Sultan Mehmed II (Conqueror) and Suleiman I (Lawgiver) as their Golden Age in the Ottoman Empire. Except for minor incidents, they faced nothing negative.

Joseph Nasi was a Jewish diplomat and administrator, for example. Joseph Nasi, known as João Micas in Portuguese and the nephew of Dona Gracia Mendes Nasi, was one of the most influential figures in the Ottoman Empire under Suleiman I and Selim II. He was the Sultan's financial advisor.

Another example: Abraham Salomon Camondo was born and raised in Istanbul as the child of a Sephardic family expelled from Spain and later arrived in Ottoman lands and would become a banker and community leader who would serve both his community and the Ottoman administration until the age of 83, when he left Istanbul. He would play a pivotal role in the transition of Istanbul's financiers from being money changers to bankers, help Galata become a modern financial centre, and finance a large part of the Ottoman army's expenses during the Crimean War. He would also go down in history as someone who, thanks to his close relations with the Grand Viziers, regulated the relations between his community and the Ottoman administration. He would become a founder of modern business life by building famous inns in various parts of Istanbul, and he would put his signature on some works that significantly contributed to the urban architecture of Istanbul. Abraham would die in Paris, where he spent his last years, and upon his will, his body would be buried in the mausoleum he had built in Haskoy with a great ceremony attended by Ottoman rulers. (Source: Daily Şalom)

The language of the community is Ladino. They struggle to keep their language alive for their generations. Their richness of mind and the significance they place on education and renewal make the Jewish community successful in commerce as in many other fields. In other words, groups with members attached to one another, support one another, and complement one another's shortcomings, can move towards a better world despite all their flaws, shortcomings, and oppression.

"The poet's poem is his mind, and the architect's work is actually himself," says Emerson.

Our human journey continues towards a destination where we will be remembered for what we have done and experienced. Our starting point will be to meet on the common denominator of world citizenship, sit, discuss, and convene unconditionally and without expectations.

# THE POWER OF INNOCENCE

**T**rue evil leaves us speechless, the only thing we can say is "This should never have happened". (Hannah Arendt)

Slander and lies are like thunder; they are very loud, frightening but ineffective. Innocence is like lightning, by the time we hear its sound, it has already reached its destination.

We know we are innocent, but we cannot prove our innocence.

Innocence bears strength. A hundred thousand tongues challenge sins and evil. Truth also has its strength. A hundred thousand tongues defy lies.

It is said that one should be afraid of a person who has lost everything, for a person who has nothing left to lose is a fearless person. People who have had everything taken from them unjustly, who have nothing left but their innocence and virtue, are also fearless. Let those who reign over all injustice and injustice be afraid!

Our history does not go linear, we experience events in a circular fashion. Even though the actors and the stage change, negative emotions and evil do not. Emotions such as jealousy, greed for power, partiality and ambition caused tens of thousands of lives while the Companions of the Holy Prophet (PBUH) were still alive. Similarly, what was done to the believers, Prophet 'Isa (peace be upon him) and his apostles during the Roman period never changed. Today it may be a feast for some and tomorrow it will be mourning for others...

In the miracle of life, the Creator has actually hidden a great patience, an elixir of endurance and a talisman, providing we use these properly. Let's use this elixir in the places where events hurt and bleed us. The love in our essence contains these medicines and remedies. As long as we do not contaminate them with hatred, jealousy, and anger ...

Suffering whips up the will to struggle. Difficulties which we do not wish to visit us and do not even think about increase our resistance in life. If one can also add gratitude and thankfulness to patience, they undoubtedly win difficult tests.

Sometimes a person clings to life with a flower in their prison ward, sometimes with a friendly greeting, sometimes hoping the evil done to them will be accountable before the law...

Compassion and love are an inexhaustible source, a cascade. Conscience is an infallible guide. Those who represent relative goodness have always existed and will always exist. Heroes who defy evil, too.

In this period, the peoples of countries like Turkey, Afghanistan, Syria, and East Turkistan are undergoing immense suffering. Homes are broken, lives are broken. Unfortunately, it is a period when cruel and despotic rulers who rewrite the book of evil are in demand.

There are two billion Muslims in this world. And it is in their lands where the suffering is typically concentrated. Geography is not destiny, but people cannot demonstrate the will and effort to make this change. Yet, the presence of the good and those who stand against evil in these countries bears more value.

"Our dreams are where our fears live," says Shirin Neshat. We live on days when our dreams are intertwined with our fears. We live on days when pain brings us together, when we are given the opportunity to share in the suffering of people from other social groups.

We believe in the power of innocence. We take refuge in the persuasive power of innocence and in the Owner of True Power and Might to the extent we can feel our helplessness down to our bones.

I believe that those who will build the future will be those who obtain their power from the right, not from the might. I know we took part in reconstruction in several periods in history when we were considered to be over, and we built civilizations. I know people who speak about hope in the darkest episodes of history, who make moves, and who are strong in goodness and hope. I read in the pages of history about people who do not give up, do not lose heart, and do not lose their innocence and fail in their struggle against evil. For me, nationality and colour have no importance. I accept those who salute hope, have adopted goodness as their motto, and continue on their way with virtue, wisdom, love of truth and justice as my own or I deem myself as one of them.

I deem it a blessing to be on the side of the innocent even if they lose, on the side of the good sworn to goodness even if they see evil, and on the side of those who follow the truth despite everything. And I know the number of those who are committed to this truth is not small at all!

"Those who sought truth by living outside their heart have always remained in darkness." says philosopher and writer Nurettin Topçu.

# BECOMING A REFUGEE AND PUSHBACKS

"We are most tired of understanding" Fernando Pessoa

The definition of refugee is someone who has been forced to flee his or her country because of persecution, war, or violence. Becoming a refugee; having to leave your homeland, taking refuge at the mercy of another country... waiting to be understood, and having your minimum human rights taken away.

The people of Greece have been truehearted so far. They have hosted tens of thousands of people fleeing the persecution of the regime in Turkey. Many refugees who crossed over to Europe miss their days in Greece and put their memories into writing. They had also mobilized for the affectees of the forest fires in Greece.

Unfortunately, unpleasant incidents happened recently. On June 23, 2021, Amnesty International published its report on pushbacks. Titled, "Greece: Violence, Lies and Pushbacks", the report focuses primarily on the illegal operations in the Evros region on the land border between Greece and Turkey. Amnesty International's report contains new evidence of torture, ill-treatment and illegal pushbacks of refugees and migrants.

Amnesty says pushbacks are not limited to border areas. People are also being apprehended and detained as far away as 700 kilometres inside the border of mainland Greece before being illegally transferred to the Evros region for extradition to Turkey. In February and March 2020, Greece violently pushed back refugees and migrants in response to Turkey's unilateral opening of its land borders. The new report, documenting the events between June and December 2020, shows that human rights violations at

Greece's borders have become an established practice.

Ankara launched a large-scale crackdown on dissent after the coup, dismissing over 150,000 government personnel with statutory decrees and arresting tens of thousands of people for alleged links to the Gülen Movement and the pro- Kurdish opposition. Besides the thousands imprisoned, thousands of Gülen Movement participants and Kurdish activists have been forced to flee Turkey to evade government repression. The threat to dissidents in Turkey seeking safe haven in Europe makes the alleged conduct of the Greek authorities a violation of the principle of non- refoulement enshrined in Article 33(1) of the 1951 UN Convention: "No Contracting State shall refuse to return a refugee because of his race, religion, nationality, membership of a particular social group or political opinion." Greece has toughened its migration policy since conservative Prime Minister Kyriakos Mitsotakis came to power in 2019.

Former TRT employee Ertan R., who fled to Greece while on trial over alleged membership in a so-called terror organization, said he was ill-treated by the Greek police for hours. Ertan R. stated that his personal belongings and identity card were confiscated by the Greek border security. He was not processed and was sent to Turkey via Egyptian human traffickers.

Stating he was treated inhumanely during the few hours he stayed in Greece, Ertan R. said, "I have no regrets about my escape attempt. My real regret is that I was treated like a dog when I crossed to the Greek side. The Greeks did not take any official action against us. They unofficially sent us back to Turkey. They seized our personal belongings. They even strip searched the women in our group. We stayed in Greece for hours and the officials did not meet our basic needs. The police officers' faces were covered. This was why we could not even see their faces." Unlike other refugees being pushed back, the biggest problem here is that Gülenists will be tortured and sent to prison if they are returned to Turkey.

Let me conclude my article with a heart-breaking photo frame from this period of persecution which will not be easily erased from my memory: Imagine a father; on his shoulder is the lifeless body of his wife who had died of a heart attack while trying to cross the border... next to him are two confused and frightened girls trying to understand what happened.

My call to people of all religions, nationalities and races who believe in conscience, justice, coexistence, equality and who have not lost these values: Let us not surrender this earth, from where we have nowhere else to go, to evildoers.

# WHAT IS BEING DONE
# TO ADDRESS
# HUMAN RIGHTS VIOLATIONS?

Especially since July 15, 2016, coup attempt, there has been a massive and mass violation of human rights in Turkey. The incision of injustice seems beyond repair, as it gets larger every day. The number of people who demand justice and not receive it exceeds millions. Some lost their jobs, some their freedom, some their lives, and some were tortured. The number of forced migrants from Turkey to abroad has reached hundreds of thousands. In all countries, migrants and asylum seekers struggle with myriad hardships such as holding on to life, learning the language, integrating into education and culture, and acclimatizing with the weather and environment.

Plus, their longing for Turkey and their relatives ...

Violations of rights, persecutions, efforts to access justice, and the search for justice and equality continue feverishly. Victims seeking their rights take several initiatives within the framework of human rights, incessantly and legitimately at all times. Some of these efforts are in Turkey and some are abroad.

What are being done? What have been done so far? Let us quote some of these activities, known on social media and announced to the public on websites, in the safe hands of the following lines and as a note to history:

On daily basis, accounts like Odak Dünyam @odakdunyam, Avrupa Adalet İnsiyatifi (European Justice Initiative), Tutsak Bebekler (Prisoner Babies), Tutuklu Hastalar (Prisoner Patients), Cezaevi İhlalleri (Prison Violations), Biten Hayatlar (Finished Lives), Kaybedilen Hayatlar (Lost Lives), and Birlikte Yaşama ve Özgürlük (Coexistence and Freedom) announce hashtags and rights violations.

There are prominent associations and platforms which constantly put human rights violations on the agenda like Solidarity with Others in Belgium, HRD and Action in Germany, AST in the United States, SCF Stockholm Center for Freedom in Sweden, Human Rights Solidarity HR in London, England besides several others in France, Spain, Portugal, and the Netherlands. Violations of rights like enforced disappearances, torture, passport revocations are reported.

The Solidarity with Others Association in Belgium prepares memory centres and databases so one day, when the rule of law returns, those who have been wronged can claim their rights from the violators.

Tenkil Museum exhibits the belongings and stories of the

oppressed who lost their lives under persecution by the regime in Turkey. The museum hosts a database of over 700 victims who died during the tenkil (banishment and extermination) process. This mobile museum in Germany fulfils a crucial mission.

NGOs opened by journalists such as the Germany-based IJA International Journalists Association and social media accounts opened by diplomats and members of the judiciary dismissed from public employment via statutory decrees constantly provide a balm to the victimized and those seeking justice.

These purpose-founded organizations submit monthly reports to institutions such as the European Union, the US Senate, Amnesty International, the European Court of Human Rights, and share these reports on their websites and social media accounts.

Turkey Tribunal is a body made up of retired diplomats and members of the judiciary who worked in the European Union, the European Parliament, or the European judiciary. They examine the human rights and civil rights violations in Turkey. For this purpose, they convene in different European countries and share their recommendations and reports with the public and the official authorities. It is a civil initiative formed by the efforts of European politicians and academics sensitive about human rights violations. They continue to seek rights for the Kurds, the Alevis, the participants of the Hizmet Movement and the minorities in Turkey.

Humanitarian assistance organizations such as Time to Help continue their work to provide relief to the victimized.

Short films, songs, and documentaries are made. Stories of oppression and the quest for justice are written. Publishing houses like Crab Publishing publish digital books as a civil initiative under different categories. Crab Publishing continues its works with 113 books and 62 authors. The publication house has published 56 books on human rights violations to date. Cizlavet Culture and Art Platform trains budding writers, provides a platform to experienced authors, and is a brand-new voice and breath through the tongue of art and culture.

Personal petitions are submitted, and prospective lawsuits are initiated at the European Court of Human Rights.

The Refugee Communication and Support Centre under the Peaceful Actions Platform (@4PeacefulAction) supports the victimized in issues such as passport cancellations, deportations, red notices, and extradition requests.

Thousands of volunteers living in Europe came together in Strasbourg on Friday, June 24, 2022, to raise the voices of the elderly people, pregnant women, babies, and all oppressed people subjected to human rights violations in Turkey, tortured, kidnapped, imprisoned in prisons, to be heard by the ECHR (European Court of Human Rights). The event was organized by 24 civil society organizations and Peaceful Actions Platform with the hashtag #JusticeForALLinTurkey and the slogans "Justice for all" and "Justice delayed is not justice".

Several civil initiatives can be noted here. Personal efforts shown by concerned individuals like Ömer Faruk Gergerlioğlu, Former NBA player Enes Kanter, Hüda Kaya, Kazım Güleçyüz, Sezgin Tanrıkulu, Ahmet Altan, Cemre Birand, Natali Avazyan, Zülfü Livaneli, Ahmet Nesin, Eser Karakaş, Dr. Şebnem Korur Fincancı, Eren Keskin who support the quest for justice without questioning the victims' affiliation, are surely admirable.

The famous British philosopher Thomas Hobbes' Leviathan, the dragon state, continues to devour its own children, forge absolute sovereignty, and disregard individual rights. No one is safe until democracy and rule of law are restored.

# Part Two

# OUR STORIES

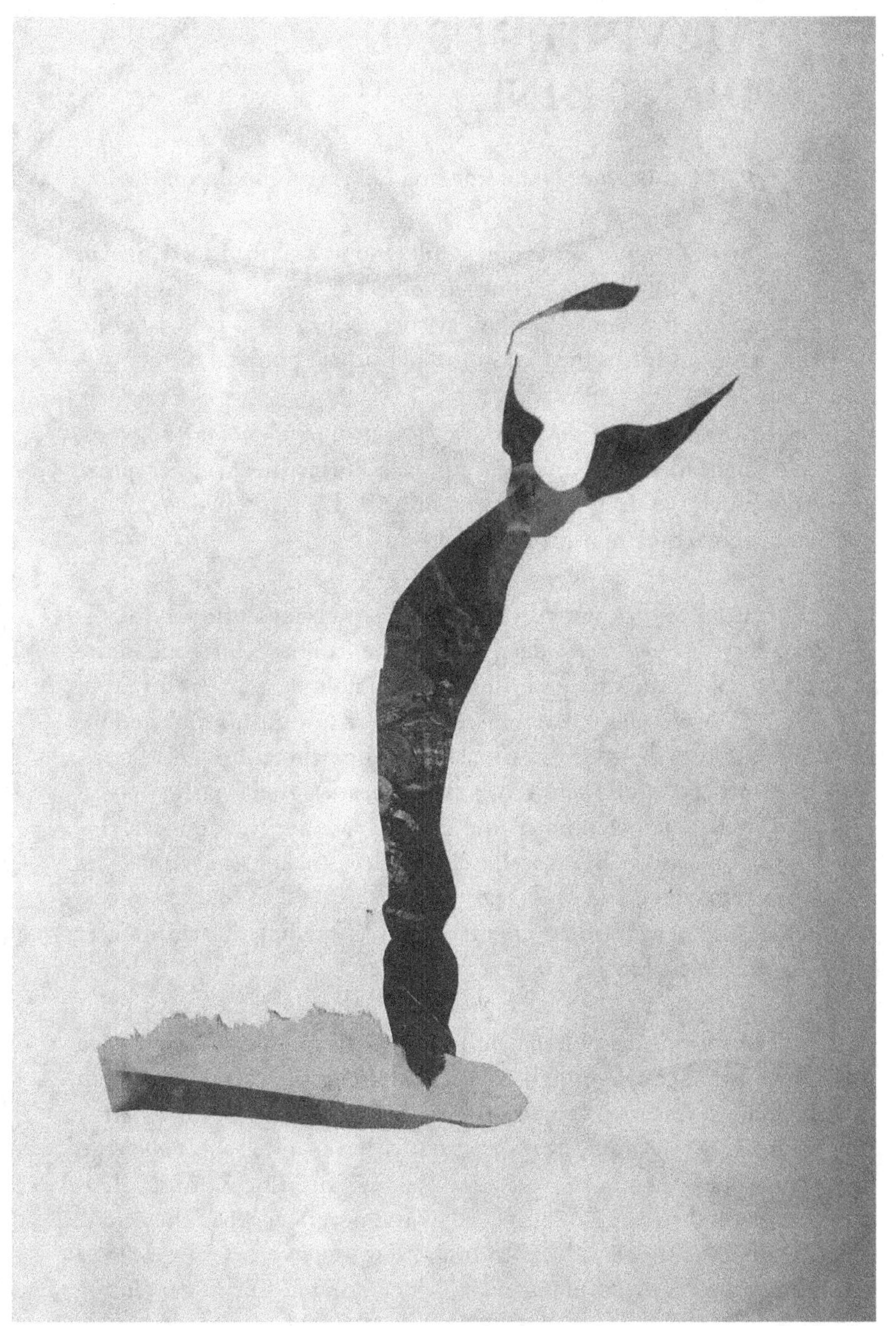

# THE VIRTUOUS HEART: HRANT DINK

Conscience is the sine qua non of an intellectual.

We lost Hrant Dink who was a Turkish-Armenian intellectual, editor-in-chief of Agos, journalist and columnist on Wednesday, January 19, 2007, on a cold Istanbul day, a day added to the dark pages of Turkish political history.

In today's Turkey, in an atmosphere where hatred, marginalization and overbearing Jacobinism are at their peak, how much we need the conscientious and enlightened ideas and courageous breath of people like Hrant...

It is an unfortunate period during which revolutionary bigots or religious bigots recklessly push the country into indefinite black holes. The disappointing thing is neither group is aware of their bigotry and so blame it all on the false dreams and fictions they built in their minds. The shallow interpretations and know-it-all attitudes of even those you consider the smartest reveal the intellectual vacuum in the country. Conscience plays a role ahead of reason. Because if the intellect makes one's injustices seem reasonable and one's betrayals seem innocent and tell one to remain silent against the cruelties one has facilitated, that intellect is then useless having lost its conscience.

How exquisitely Hrant Dink depicts the mosaic of Turkey with these sentences: "I don't know if you are aware of this... We can no longer trade jokes with one another, we have become rather wary. Yet how much fun we used to have, didn't we, when we would be deep in conversation telling Turkish, Kurdish, Laz, Jewish, and Armenian jokes? We would never get hurt. These were common products of our common culture. We would modify a Kurd into a Laz, a Jew into an Armenian, and so on, depending on the occasion. Unfortunately, our differences have been so much demonized that we are even afraid to tell jokes to one another each other..."

The way to talk about our issues in a constructive manner is once again is through the principles of universal law based on conscience and the democratization of democracy through freedom of expression. Without applying universal principles of law, equality and human rights revert to the notion that George Orwell ironized in Animal Farm: "Everyone is equal, but some are more equal".

Agos Newspaper Editor-in-Chief Hrant Dink was commemorated on the 15th anniversary of his assassination. Speaking with sobs, Hrant's spouse Rakel Dink said, "Don't be a partner in the fruitless deeds of darkness." She was right; those who rely on their current power and reign thinking it will never end continue to commit many crimes against humanity. Even young children committing suicide cannot stop their lust for crime. The opposition groups who stand by and not speak out against these wrongdoings are also involved in the crimes against humanity.

If you judge and humiliate the diversities and different identities you live with, this is racism and the world's greatest crime against humanity, Hrant used to say. Like what Kemalist, religious and ultra-nationalist groups are doing to Hizmet and its participants as well as to the Kurds and the Armenians. We are the other of the other...

Hilal Nesin recently tweeted the truth that needs to be exclaimed: "How unwise you are. Do you think I won't share about the victimized when you call them 'F. TOists' or 'those from the Community?' I don't care what you call them. I neither believed in the coup claimed by Erdoğan and his gang, nor did I consider those he labelled terrorists as terrorists. I am one of those who were not deceived."

One does not become Hrant Dink by reading Spinoza's Ethics and referring to Emmanual Levinas on ethics and the other. To be Hrant Dink, shouldn't you put your conscience on the line and stand by those who are in search of truth and justice with no ifs or buts?

Hrant Dink completed his life as a timid but free dove in the city, among the crowds. Those who want to silence him and the likes of him should know that truths and ideas wear wings and continue their journey even after centuries; you cannot kill ideas and the conscience!

Let's end with what Turkish musician Sezen Aksu says:

You can't kill me

I have a voice, an instrument, a word

When I say I, I'm everybody.

# A COLOSSUS:
# YUSUF PEKMEZCI

Businessmen Yusuf Pekmezci is a lofty soul who is self-reliantly aspired for serving the humanity. He alone is the proof and chronicle of the Hizmet Movement. Yusuf Bekmezci was born in 1939 in the Üzümlü village of Beysehir district in Konya province. In 1951, he went to Izmir to attend the primary school. He fulfilled his military service in Isparta. Afterwards, he engaged in trade at his store selling kitchenware and porcelain in Izmir. He married and had 15 grandchildren from three daughters and one son.

He met Fethullah Gülen during Gülen's first years in Izmir. He assumed duties on the board of the Kestanepazarı student dormitory. He was a philanthropist. One of his memories in the Bozyaka dormitory from the early years of the Hizmet Movement is evidence of the heart Yusuf Bekmezci had. Due to some severe problems and his circle of friends' lack of understanding about his vision, Fethullah Gülen Hodjaefendi decided to leave and packed his suitcase. Witnessing this, Halim Baba immediately rushed to Yusuf Bekmezci and said, "Only you can stop Hodjaefendi!" Yusuf Bekmezci quickly arrived at the Bozyaka dormitory, threw himself in front of Hodjaefendi and exclaimed, "Before you, I used to sleep peacefully; you have long disturbed our routine! I cannot sleep anymore thinking the problems of people and our generation, this is the first time we have experienced such a thing. Now you cannot leave us with these troubles and go away!" with a stern expression and convinced Hodjaefendi to stay.

### A pioneer for the Hizmet Movement in Kazakhstan

In the early years of Hizmet, he was involved in every significant activity and was a pioneer. He was also among the firsts to frequent the conversations made by Fethullah Gülen Hodjaefendi in coffeehouses in Izmir. He was one pioneer to go to Kazakhstan with four Hizmet-inspired colleagues in 1991. In his own words, "We were four ignorant people" says Yusuf Bekmezci. He spent 15 years full of action and productivity in the land of the Kazakhs. As soon as they arrived in Kazakhstan, they visited the Ministry of Education and were soon indulged in an ardent activity to open a school. They took Ministry officials to Turkey and showed them the dormitories and private schools opened by the Hizmet Movement. They took the first steps to open schools compatible with the official Turkish curriculum and the Kazakh history and culture. He reluctantly returned to Turkey, leaving behind 28 schools and numerous graduates.

The current events in Kazakhstan, Russia's constant interventions and the fact there is still no full transition to democracy are saddening. I believe if the Hizmet Schools are sufficiently supported, the fate of the Central Asia will change. People like Yusuf Bekmezci have no material expectations, they are not pragmatic. Their only interest is to please the Almighty and seek His divine approval, to unite people around love and the ideal of facilitating the future generations to live in a better and more moral society.

### School Man

"If you really love your Creator, take a sincere look at every human being! Do not break hearts and accept people as they are! We have accepted both the communists and the atheists as our own children," says this altruistic man with a beautiful heart. Having visited 30 countries and almost every province in Turkey, this man, who personified this cause of education and may be termed a 'School Man', spent his life in pursuit of supporting and providing opportunities for young people. He struggled to offer peace and happiness projects to humanity. The likes of Yusuf Bekmezci are the infatuated ones who sing the folk songs of humanity on desolate mountain tops. They are both mature individuals who exist as themselves and convey their own embroidery into the present, and team men who pave the way for those who come after them. They are the ones who discovered early on that it is possible to become an ocean from a droplet, and therefore to attain immortality. They are sincere souls who have crossed hills on the path to self-understanding and are dedicated to understanding others. They are the true rich who realize that wealth is not about amassing and hoarding wealth, but generously spending it on people.

Over 82 years old and suffering from Alzheimer's, hypertension, amnesia, osteoporosis, and severe memory loss, Yusuf Bekmezci was detained by today's power worshippers in the School of Joseph bearing the name, Buca Kırıklar Prison. Having been deprived of his freedom and most basic human rights, he was subjected to persecution at its peak. Yes, the maxim "Power can make people incoherent and devour their own moral values" once again proves true. Most politicians of this period know Yusuf Pekmezci so well; they dined with him several times at his home. Yet, when he was in intensive care, they did not help him to be released despite all his illnesses! He died languishing in a prison before he could regain his freedom, merely because of negligence. This is also the officials' misfortune.

Let us conclude with these words of 'Mevlana' Jalaluddin Rumi:

"Your wounds are the spots where the light enters inside."

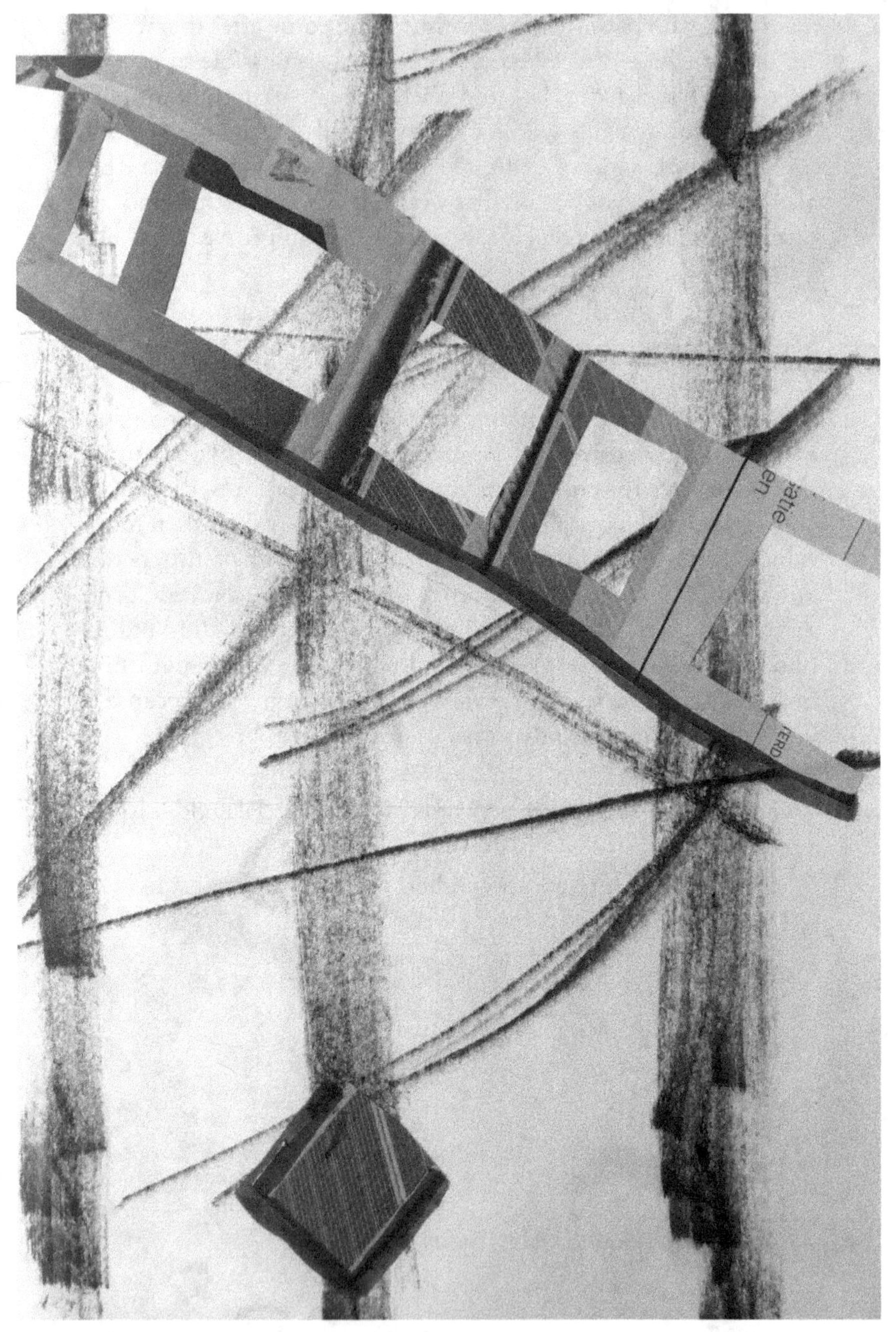

# STORIES OF THE NEW EUROPEANS

Turkish people are Asian and a little bit European. We reflect the affiliation described by Amin Maalouf in Fatal Identities. Even though we migrated to the West, there is still an aspect of the East that attracts us, that is in our genetic codes.

We have negative aspects like violence, anger, militarism, marginalization, oppressing, lack of tolerance, and being upset by one another's achievements.

We also have positive aspects like generosity, hospitality, resilience, quick integration into settings, and the sense of sacrifice when one believes in something.

We are no strangers to the West. We have been migrating to the West for about 60 years.

The contributions made by the participants of the Hizmet Movement, who arrived in Europe during the last six years after the July 15 coup attempt and now form a part of the Hizmet Movement, to the society and their condition will be better understood in near future. More psychosociological, cultural and sociological articles will be written, and research will be conducted on this subject. In recent years, highly qualified and highly educated immigrants have arrived in Europe from Turkey.

Hizmet Movement volunteers who migrate to Europe are generally liberal and conservative. However, it is inconceivable they remain indifferent to socialist parties which emphasize immigrant rights. They can also be defined as concerned conservatives. Meanwhile it can generally be said they have a social structure that is open to modernization, innovation and technology. Especially the young generations of the Hizmet Movement receive education in European universities and grow up as better equipped citizens of the world. Yet another significant aspect here is that the emerging youth can continue their lives without severing themselves from their own spiritual and ethical values.

Integration is not a fast-emerging phenomenon. Every nation has experienced similar stories after migrating to different countries for compelling reasons. You can observe citizens from Lebanon, Pakistan, Bangladesh, Syria, Afghanistan, Iraq, Korea, the Baltics, and various African countries in Europe. They all have different stories of survival. One of my beloved elders used to say that we, as a nation, are like those who try to get on the bus last; wherever we go, we see that other nations have already arrived and settled in those lands before us.

Some who arrived and settled in Europe as workers from the 1960s and onwards have later become self-employed.

Volunteers who met and supported the Hizmet Movement in the following years have also contributed to their host society. The lives of the immigrants who arrived and settled in these countries years ago and the positive or negative impacts they have left on today's Europe and immigration policies cannot be denied.

However, it must be quite difficult for immigrants, whether they arrived earlier or recently and who watch the Turkish TV channels, are unaware of the culture and the language of their host country and remain in contact only with people who speak their mother language, to rid themselves of ghettoization and contribute to their host society. Although the articles and studies published about the Hizmet Movement in Europe are positive in terms of the participants' good conduct, non-violence and rapid integration, it is not disregarded that the Hizmet is noticeably introverted.

This period has also an advantage, though: In countries like the Netherlands, Spain and Germany, the state centrally allots the refugees all over the country. This way, ghettoization can be prevented, and faster localization and integration can be facilitated.

When we go through the immigrant stories of other nations and the experiences of people like Kahlil Jibran, we see that it is difficult to hold on to life in a new country, to hold fast, not to break away from one's values and roots, and to love and contribute to the host society. It is essential to overcome crucial difficulties and put up a struggle.

Let me share a few stories as examples. Let's not exaggerate these stories, yes, but let's not ignore them either:

Mr. Murat, a forced migrant to the Netherlands, attracts the attention of local authorities through the education program he and his fellow refugees prepare for the refugee children in the camp in three months. His letter of thanks to Utrecht Mayor Sharon Dijksma became a phenomenon in the city after the mayor posted it on her Instagram account.

Immigrants living in Europe for years are also now reaping the rewards of their achievements.

Basri Dogan, a journalist who moved to the Netherlands years ago and was awarded the Royal Dutch Prize, is a commendable integration story.

Sema Aydoğan, President of the Fedactio Dialogue Platform in Belgium, was voted as one of the "100 Most Influential Women in Brussels" for the activities she organized during the coronavirus pandemic. This is a distinctive story worth noting.

In the United States of America, we witness the days Enes Kanter Freedom – as an immigrant US citizen – is nominated for the Nobel Peace Prize as a Human Rights Activist for his steadfast stance against China's persecution of the Uyghurs.

"Thanks to our heritage from the past and what we have witnessed, we will find the courage to resist and continue to resist under conditions we cannot imagine now. We will learn to wait in solidarity." (Berger)

# REBEL TURNED HERO DIPLOMAT

" **W**hat kind of a place is this world where you have to be crazy to do the right thing?" *(Aristides de Sousa Mendes)*

Heroes emerge in difficult and feared times. Times of war and dictatorship are when the initiatives and the hearts of men of duty like Emile Zola are in demand.

Dictators build a world for themselves surrounded by walls of fear. They think they are unreachable, that they are chosen and that they know best. Yet, they are lonely and cowardly.

Aristides de Sousa Mendes (July 18, 1885 - April 3, 1954) was a prestigious Portuguese diplomat who saved 30,000 lives from the Holocaust by hastily issuing visas for both individuals and families. Between June 16 and 23, 1940, Aristides de Sousa Mendes disobeyed orders imposed by dictator Salazar and followed the dictates of his conscience.

Aristides de Sousa Mendes do Amaral e Abranches was born on July 19, 1885, in Cabanas de Viriato, near Viseu. He is the son of Maria Angelina Ribeiro de Abranches and judge José de Sousa Mendes. With his twin brother César, he graduated in Law from the University of Coimbra at 22.

In 1908 he married his cousin Angelina, with whom he would have 14 children. He began his diplomatic career at a young age and in 1910 became the Consul for Demerara in British Guiana. He was the consul in British Guiana, Zanzibar, Brazil (Curitiba and Porto Alegre), the United States (San Francisco and Boston), Spain (Vigo), Luxembourg, Belgium and finally France (Bordeaux). He was a family man. He was a family man who never abandoned his wife and children; he provided his children academic training as well as art and music lessons. One of his sons said one day: "We had an actual chamber orchestra in our house, and we regularly invited people to our concerts. We played Chopin, Mozart, Bach, Beethoven, besides the compositions of several others."

During the Second World War, Portugal under Salazar's dictatorship was a so-called "neutral" nation, although it was openly and unofficially pro-Hitler. The Portuguese government issued a mandatory "Circular 14" to all its diplomats, rejecting refugees – including Jews, Russians, and stateless persons – a safe haven. However, a certain man defied these terrible orders and, by resonating his conscience, saved 30,000 people from certain death.

Aristides Sousa Mendes was severely punished by Salazar, who dismissed him from his official post and deprived him of any means of livelihood, as Sousa Mendes had 15 children who were blacklisted and prevented by the regime from taking admission in universities. As the Nazi threat permeated and the persecution of thousands of Jews in Europe was intensified, taking shape in startling dimensions, thousands of Jewish refugees in Bordeaux gathered outside the consulates of Portugal and Spain to obtain visas and to escape imminent death. Spain denied visas to the Jewish refugees. The only hope lay in the Portuguese consulate.

On June 16, 1940, Aristides de Sousa Mendes, the Portuguese consul in Bordeaux, met Rabbi Kruger, who had fled occupied Poland. Sousa Mendes promised to do everything in his power to convince the Lisbon government led by Salazar. That night, he welcomed Rabbi Kruger into his home. On the morning of June 17, 1940, Lisbon refused to issue visas to the Jewish refugees, but unexpectedly Aristides de Sousa Mendes informed the rabbi that he would issue the visas because he knew the refugees were condemned to death in atrocious concentration camps.

Sousa Mendes had his family home – Casa do Passal in Cabanas de Viriato, Viseu – mortgaged by the bank and eventually sold it to pay off debts. In those days of hardship, the Lisbon Jewish Association was the only organization that provided food and medical assistance to the Sousa Mendes family. Aristides de Sousa Mendes died in poverty on April 3, 1954, but until his last breath he sought justice for his deeds.

Between June 17 and 19, the Portuguese consul and his two children worked non-stop without even a meal break. During those three days, 30,000 visas were issued, contrary to the explicit orders of dictator António de Oliveira Salazar. In contrast, the Portuguese consulates in Bayonne and Hendaye had obeyed Salazar; however, when Aristides de Sousa Mendes visited these cities in person, more Portuguese visas were issued. Sousa Mendes was aware of the consequences of his actions, yet he followed the dictates of his own conscience. On June 24, 1940, Aristides de Sousa Mendes received a telegram from Salazar ordering him to return to Lisbon and explain his act of disobedience. Aristides de Sousa Mendes was not only expelled but was also denied any privilege. Despite his 30-year diplomatic career, his children were banned from university education and the Sousa Mendes family rapidly lost everything, including their family home. The Jewish Community of Lisbon provided the family with shelter and food and helped some of their children to move to the United States or Canada.

The first recognition arrived from Israel in 1966 when Aristides de Sousa Mendes received the "International Integrity Award". In 1986, the United States Congress issued a proclamation in honour of Sousa Mendes' heroic action. Later, he was ultimately recognized by Portugal, where the erstwhile President Mário Soares apologized to the Sousa Mendes family and the Portuguese Parliament posthumously promoted him to the rank of ambassador. Sousa Mendes' face were printed on stamps in several countries. *(Source: Center Portugal)*

*"He who saves one life saves all mankind." (A.S. Mendes)*

# DON'T LOOK UP

"The further a society moves away from the truth, the more it hates those who tell the truth." (George Orwell)

Don't Look Up is Adam McKay's new movie released with an impressive cast.

The plot of the movie is briefly this: Kate Dibiasky (Jennifer Lawrence) is a PhD student at the Michigan State University. She discovers a huge comet approaching the Earth, threatening to end all life in exactly 6 months and 14 days.

She and Professor Randall Mindy (Leonardo DiCaprio) visit the White House to brief President Janie Orlean (Meryl Streep). They tell her about the impending doom of the world and say, "We all are going to die!" This is what they get as an answer: "Don't look up!"

The movie is about the hardship of believing that carefree politicians will do the right thing even when the end of the world is near. It says, "Don't look up! Close your eyes! Don't see the reality!" The movie tells us that even when there is a fast-approaching comet to bring the end of the world, there will always be politicians who calculate the ways to monetize the minerals in that meteorite; politicians who disregard your life, have recessed consciences, and have become lapdogs for politics.

The world is in a state of meanness and the non-humanistic and inhuman aspects of populism have invaded every aspect of our lives. One message given in the movie is that the giant egos and the privileged rich, who do not care if the world burns, cause all this. Their reckless flight into space is an indication of this.

Rich people, celebrities, opinion leaders, writers, intellectuals, and politicians in every country of the world experience a solemn test phase. We are sitting for the test of remaining human, of not losing our conscience. The test of not forgetting the real questions we need to ask, of not losing the answers which make up the meaning of life... The test of not betraying our existence...

Those who are pushed back at the Greek border are also deprived of their most humane and legal right to asylum! EU officials who stand by and watch these incidents too give a test of humanity. Either they will say "Don't look up and close your eyes to reality" or they will accept the facts and seek solutions.

From a different perspective, we can also link the movie "Don't Look Up" with the reasons for the battery and detention of the Bosphorus University protesters: Not looking down! The police had forced the marching students to "look down!" and detained those who did not comply by beating them.

While human rights violations peak in Turkey, while Turkey tops the bill in all international reports and is on the red lists for money laundering, and while people are merely abandoned to die in prisons, the authorities and those who hold power nowadays will either listen to the voice of their conscience or will remain spectators to the apocalypse.

As I write these lines, in these minutes when the night's darkness changes to the dawn's light, I have been shaken by the news of the death of Leyla Kurt, the wife of Mr. Yusuf Kurt, the school principal with whom I had worked in Madagascar. Mrs. Leyla had fought against cancer for a long time. Her husband Yusuf Kurt has been in prison for five years. He was not given the right to probation albeit his sentence was over. Mrs. Leyla's clear conscience could not cope with the responsibility of her three children and the sad events that had taken place.

Goethe says, "The world is a hell for sensitive souls."

People like Mrs. Leyla are the conscience of society. No matter if you exclude them or not accept them, Leyla Kurt and her peers are like Kate Dibiasky and Professor Randal Mindy; people with a clear conscience who shout out the truth, exclaiming that a meteor is approaching to hit the earth and that we all will perish without exception.

# GARİBE GEZER AND HALİME GÜLSU

G aribe Gezer and Halime Gülsu are two lives I am ashamed of my humanity for being a stakeholder of the same period, for being a mere bystander to their deaths. Garibe Gezer, whom I heard about in the media and was very saddened when I read her story, is first and foremost a human, a woman, a citizen. She was born in 1994 in Dargeçit, Mardin. She became a leader of a proscribed organization at a young age. Her older brother Bilal Gezer was killed by unknown assailants during the Kobane protests. When his other brother Mehmet Emin Gezer went to the District Security Directorate to call them to account for his murdered brother, an armed clash broke out and he was seriously wounded. He was then paralyzed from the waist down.

Garibe Gezer was arrested in Kütahya in 2018 and produced in court. Gezer, who was found guilty by the court, was sentenced to 28 years in prison after the initial sentence of life imprisonment. In addition, the officials launched criminal inquiries against Garibe's mother, father, siblings and nine other family members.

Beaten and dragged on the floor in Kandıra F Type Closed Prison No. 1 on May 24, Garibe Gezer was subjected to torture in the padded room and sexual torture by female guards. 28 years old Garibe first attempted suicide and later became a victim of the hostile attitude of the medical personnel at the hospital she was taken to.

Garibe did not give up and wanted to report her ordeals through letters, but her letters are seized. Saying "Let my tribulations be heard", Garibe took the opportunity of her weekly phone calls with her family to tell them all details, but this time she was put in solitary confinement for what she told. After five days in solitary confinement, Garibe explained to the prosecutor's office and the office of the judge of execution about the physical and sexual torture she had been subjected to. However, her efforts came to no fruition. Lost hopes can transform into lost lives. On December 10, Human Rights Day, she – as another female prisoner – unfortunately, took her life in her cell. She left this world with many questions and the tears of her relatives behind her...

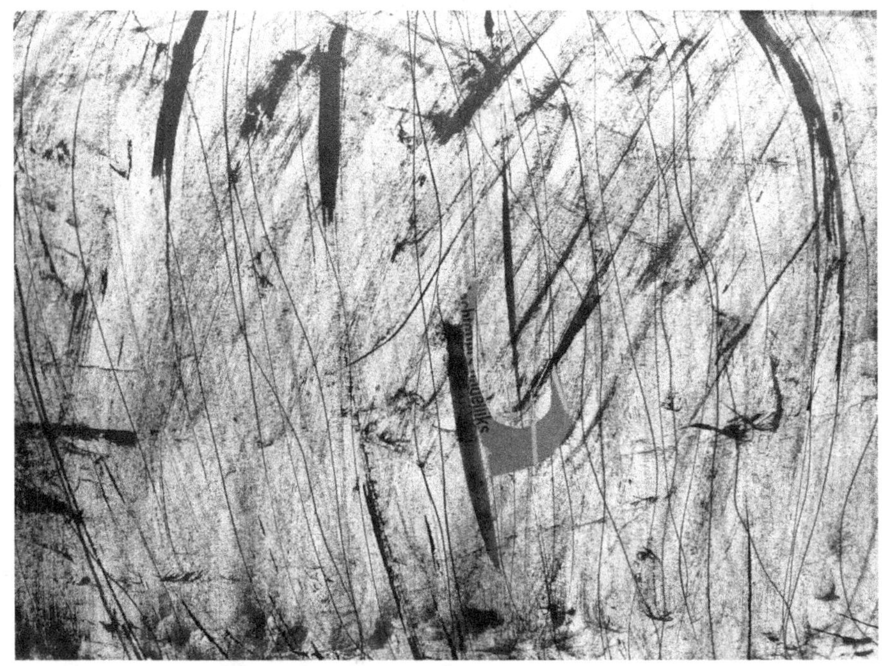

**Halime Gülsu was born in Tarsus in 1984.**

She was an English teacher, an education volunteer. Like the teachers who educated you and us... Explaining that teacher Halime spent her childhood in the village, her family also tells these with a bitter smile: "Since there was no water in the village, she used to fetch water on donkey. She loved to help her mother bake bread. We lived a hard life, and she got along well with her friends. After finishing the primary school in the village, she attended a Qur'anic school. Later, she studied at the super high school in Tarsus. In 2011, she enrolled in the Gaziantep University, Department of English Language and Literature.

After the dastardly July 15 coup attempt, she was imprisoned for selling steak tartar a la turca and providing financial aid to the victimized. She had a hard time in prison; her right to treatment was denied and she was deprived of her medication despite her terminal illness. She suffered from 'chronic systemic lupus erythematosus.'

She was one of the 21 inmates forced to stay in a 10-person prison ward. The prison officials ignored her health condition and deprived her of her most basic human rights. While awaiting trial, she was denied medication and deprived of lifesaving medical support.

In the petition she wrote four days before her death, Halime Gülsu appealed:

"I signed a paper handed to me by the police officers on duty saying they had phoned my family. However, when I met my brother after he was arrested and sent to prison, he told me he had not received any phone call back then and that he had no information about my medication. A week later, since I had been in detention, I could not receive my daily medication because I could not demand it in writing from the police officers on duty. I could not receive two doses of my medication for two weeks, even though they were available at my home. My petitions, which I cannot even remember the number of times I remarked as 'urgent' to be taken to the infirmary as per the prison rules, were not even replied and I was not taken to the infirmary. In the meantime, my illness relapsed, and I started suffering from weakness, fatigue, and joint pains. I also felt constantly nauseous. I wrote a petition again and was eventually referred by the infirmary staff to be treated at the Internal Medicine clinic of a hospital. An ambulance from the 112 Emergency Service arrived. Even though I told the paramedics about my illness, they checked my blood pressure and pulse and sent me back to my ward saying, 'We hope nothing will happen'. The prison guards thought I had been lying and they scolded me. My illness is extremely serious and fatal, and I request due process to be initiated against all concerned officials in the Mersin Security Directorate, Counter-Terrorism Unit Directorate, Tarsus Women's Closed Penal Institution, and the Tarsus State Hospital who neglected their duties in the incidents I mentioned in the petition from the day I was detained until today when I have written this petition."

Teacher Halime could no longer endure to what she had been subjected and lost her life 2 months and 10 days later. The Tarsus District Governorate did not authorize an administrative investigation into the criminal complaints filed about the death of Halime Gülsu, whose lifeless body was released from the prison where the state should have protected her. Mersin Public Prosecutor Zeki Topaloğlu closed the file, stating that no one was responsible for the death of teacher Halime Gülsu.

Despite being claimed as closed, Halime teacher's file has not yet been closed either before the law or in the Hereafter.

Many Garibes, Halimes, and children of this homeland sadly wither away one after another like autumn leaves. They leave behind their tearful, heartbroken families and relatives.

In Turkey, the winter makes itself felt on the oppressed with all its severity and every sigh under oppression is another nail in the coffin of the country. Democracy and rule of law will not return to this country until all people of conscience, especially intellectuals, speak out against human rights violations without discriminating between social backgrounds.

With so much guilt and lack of conscience, sinking to the bottom is inevitable.

# FREEDOM BEHIND BARS: İLHAN SAMİ ÇOMAK

"That age of love,

Must return, must come back. How I endured

I can never forget it again, Those fears, those worries Flew away to the skies.

A thistly thirst

Makes my veins swell.

Must return, must come back, That age of love."

*(Rimbaud)*

İlhan Çomak and I are at the same age. He is from Karlıova, Bingöl. He was imprisoned at 22, and has been longing for the sky for 27 years... I, meanwhile, have traversed three continents and lived in every shade of the sky.

After 16 days of torture, he was handed a statement and made to sign it. He was interned by the State Security Court and was sentenced to life imprisonment in 2000. When the Court of Cassation upheld his sentence, he applied to the ECHR. The ECHR ruled in 2007 that he had not received a fair trial and that he should be retried... After lengthy procedures, his sentence was upheld again by the Court of Cassation in 2018. With 27 years, he is the longest- imprisoned 'thought criminal'.

Life in prison is captivity for some and complete freedom for others. İlhan Çomak has added forte to prison poetry anthologies with his poems.

In pursuit of his innocence, he writes new poems with a brand-new spirit, announces his voice to the whole world and invites life into his cell. He has eight poetry books titled "Gitmeler Çiçek Kurusu" (Each Departure's a Dried Flower), "Açık Deniz" (Open Sea), "Günaydın Yeryüzü" (Good Morning Earth), "Kedilerin Yazdığı İlahi" (A Hymn Written by Cats), "Bir Sabah Yürüdüm" (I Walked One Morning), "Yağmur Dersleri" (Lessons of Rain), "Dicle'nin Günlüğü" (Diary of the Tigris), and "Geldim Sana" (I Came to You).

These books consist of poems penned in prison. He also clings to hope with the plant growing on the wall in the 4.5- step common area. Like a child, he rejoices at the plastic study table placed in his room after a long struggle.

He exchanges letters with European poets; half of the poems are completed by them and the other half by İlhan Çomak. He can observe life as an outsider and his poems become a source of hope for his readers far away. The more imprisoned he is, the more liberated he becomes.

Prisons have a vent to the human soul. You listen to yourself more; when you are free, you cannot turn inward that much.

"They knotted a bird in my heart.

For I learned from you that waiting is a built-in value..."
*(İlhan Sami Çomak)*

According to the IFJ International Federation of Journalists report, Turkey has the second highest number of imprisoned journalists in the world. If we want freedom, let's liberate people.

# TEACHER HIDIR

"Ask me about the misery of unfavourable fortune

Oh woe! Ask me about the torment of fortune

I well know how much I have suffered in hope

Ask me about the tribulation in uncertainty of waiting

Sundry of its atrocities have I witnessed in a day or two

Ask me about the fickle and fleeting thing called fate"

*(Ottoman Poet Nedim)*

Soldiers are martyred, aren't teachers martyred too?

Hıdır Çalka was born in Mardin to a family of seven children. He devoted himself to teaching. After graduating from the İzzet Baysal University, Department of Mathematics, he migrated to Kenya as an education volunteer. The 37-year- old devoted teacher spent 10 years in Kenya with educational activities. Later, he moved to Mogadishu with his wife and two children in pursuit of his ideals.

Mogadishu, the largest city, and capital of the eastern African country of Somalia, has been a key port city for hundreds of years thanks to its location on the shores of the Indian Ocean in the Banaadir region. After Somalia declared its independence in 1960, Mogadishu was showcased as the "White Pearl of the Indian Ocean".

Teacher Hıdır provided teaching and guidance services to the black pearls for eight months at Bedir College and Kıblenüma

Primary School opened by Turkish entrepreneurs in Mogadishu, the capital of Somalia, and touched their lives. Similar to his many friends from Anatolia who devoted themselves to education and migrated worldwide, Teacher Hıdır (originally Hızır) moved to Africa inspired by the love of inculcating universal values to hearts in need.

People in our country used to think Africa was a monobloc country. When Teacher Hıdır and the likes of him opened up to Africa, altruistic businesspeople diverted their attention to African countries. Despite a historical familiarity with North Africa, other African regions had not been known to them.

The West's discovery of Africa impacted the expanding of trade through acquiring new markets and access to spices, gold, silver, and other raw materials. In particular, the introduction of the compass, which had been used by the Chinese, in the West at the beginning of the 13th century and the subsequent development of maritime techniques initiated maritime expeditions to unknown parts of the world. The geographical explorations after 1418 were mainly motivated by economic and religious reasons. The exhaustion of gold deposits in Europe caused Europeans to turn to Africa for gold. During their expeditions to Africa, the Portuguese reached the mouth of the Senegal River in 1445. This progress and exploitation continuously increased.

People like Teacher Hıdır have gone down in African history as those who wrote the story of the white man and goodness. They took steps to contribute to changing the fortunes of the black continent and educated students.

On March 30, 2016, in the morning, he left his home in Mogadishu once more with enthusiasm. As he left, he said goodbye to his wife Mrs. Atiye and kissed and tightly hugged his two-year-old son Mehmet Akif. The school van had arrived. In the van were his fellow educators including Ms.

Kemale İsmailova, a Turkish teacher from Azerbaijan. Teacher Hıdır left his home with the hurry for catching up with his morning classes and the enthusiasm for meeting his students.

The first rays of the sun were dancing in the skies over Mogadishu when the school van moved, yet there was a whiff of sorrow in the air... Teacher Hıdır and the educators in the school van drove on, unaware of the disaster that would soon befall them. As they approached the school, near a central location, they suddenly heard gunshots. At first, they could not sense from where the sounds came.

They reluctantly reached under the seats with fear in their eyes. Soon they realized their vehicle was the target in the fusillade. In panic, they tried to get out of the vehicle.

Meanwhile, some educators had been shot. Thugs with bloodshot eyes kept on fusillading the school vehicle. Teacher Hıdır realized there was no escape from the hail of bullets. A treacherous ambush had been set up, targeting the hands holding the pen once again. His wife, children and students flashed before his eyes; his father, a shopkeeper in Istanbul, guested in his fleeting memory: "Go, my son, your students will be waiting for you there. We will come to visit you one day," his father had said to him. Teacher Hıdır had devoted his youth to education and his students. Uttering his final prayer in testimony of his Islamic faith, he breathed his last smiling in the face of death. He and his six fellow educators perished in this brutal attack. Several Somali officials and the graduates in Somalia offered condolences. People wept at his grave.

In a small newspaper article, this was written: "Hıdır Çalka, an education volunteer who lost his life in the bloody terrorist attack in Somalia, was buried in Istanbul with prayers."

No matter what happens, even if the mindsets hostile to

education and schooling resort to all kinds of dastardly acts, the likes of Teacher Hıdır and his colleagues have once again proved they will not resort to violence, and undemocratic and unlawful actions.

As said by the poet:

On the quake of your absence, the innkeeper and the inn collapsed

A house of exile's meted to the oppressed and the world's for the oppressor

Those who adore, admire, and obey you

Are dealt with a crushing test in a tunnel of troubles.

# ORHAN İNANDI AND THE SAD ESCAPES

Educator Orhan İnandı devoted his 27 years, the best years of his life to Kyrgyzstan. He is one of the pioneer educators to migrate to the Central Asia. He is a hero who devoted his life to the upbringing of the lost generations described by Cengiz Aitmatov in his book "The White Ship".

İnandı is the founder of the Sapat International Educational Institutions in Kyrgyzstan. Sapat International Educational Institutions presently have 21 schools with 9036 students. In 2002, for his contribution to the education system of the Kyrgyz Republic, he was awarded the Medal of Honour with the title "Excellence in Education of the Kyrgyz Republic" and the accompanying Certificate of Appreciation of the Kyrgyz Republic. In 2003, he was awarded the Medal of Honour. He completed his doctorate in Kyrgyzstan.

In return for all his hard work, he was abducted by thugs for political gain. Unfortunately, he was subjected to a persecution of which documents will sooner or later be produced before the law. In countries where democracy has not matured, such discrepancies between the people and the regime exist. However, the Kyrgyz people including the graduates of the schools, diplomats, and writers truthfully defend and support Orhan İnandı. This issue may be discussed more broadly, but since there are several posts and comments on social media, I will draw attention in this article to another lawlessness and banditry committed by the regime in Mali, which tries to survive through oppression.

It was late afternoon when they raided the school. It was probably the first time a truckload of soldiers had ever raided a school in this city. Mali is the eighth largest country in Africa by area. It is a West African country with a population of twenty million, mostly young people. Islam spread to the neighbouring countries from here.

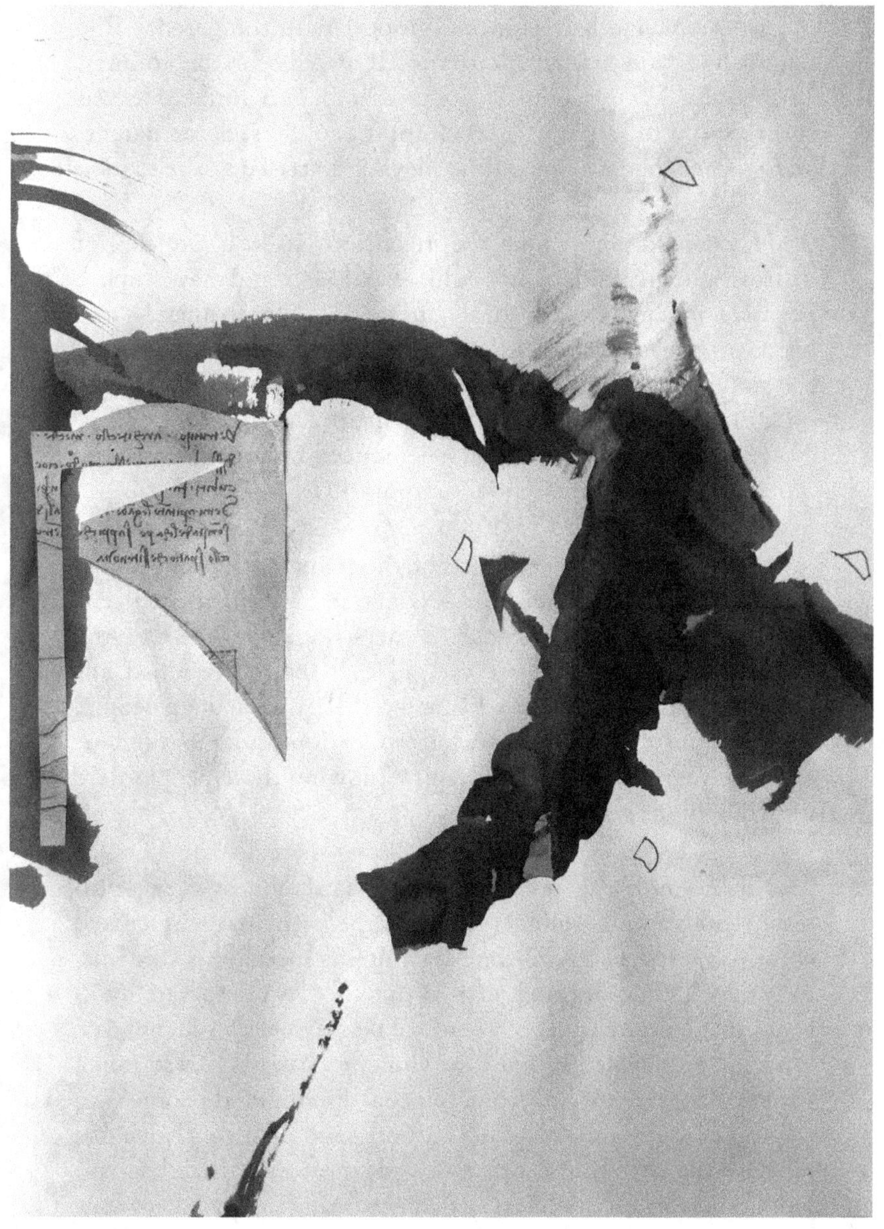

Educator Hakan had been living in Mali for six years. He was a respectable educator and administrator. The children of several ministers and prominent people of the country studied in his school. He had a sincere rapport with the parents. The school had won several international awards for the country. Mr. Hakan left his home for the school in a hurry. He was surprised by the sight of a truck full of soldiers. Some parents and teachers had also heard the news and arrived at the school.

Hakan did not think the relentless Turkish policies of distress and intimidation would reach Mali and have such a negative impact on the local authorities. Unfortunately, the black propaganda confused the minds of those who governed the state in Mali and caused some interest groups to be bought off and decide for darkening the future of the country's youth. The Turkish educators were first sentenced to house arrest. The officials also sealed the school temporarily.

Later, due to the insistence of the parents, the school was reopened. As the school year was about to start, the officials revoked the operation license of the school. On the day, the school opened, Mr. Hakan was sad that their efforts had not yielded results. The state had labelled these immaculate people, who had no other objective but education and morality for all these years, as terrorists, despite knowing these people were undeniably innocent...

Hakan took the podium, trying hard not to break into tears. Parents and students watched the principal with mixed emotions. He had a hard time starting his speech; his students, to whom he had devoted years of his life, had desperate looks begging him not to leave them. Hakan's speech did not last long: "We struggled so hard for you, and you gave us so much support. Even then, unfortunately, narrow-minded people who put their interests ahead of their country and their youth decided to close the school and deport us, disregarding these brilliant young people." The soldiers issued a warning saying, "Leave the school! On behalf of the state, we take over the school!" Hakan made a last effort to call the ministers. Unfortunately, these friends who always answered his phone calls did not answer this time. "Anyway," he thought "I will call again in the morning." Desperate, he and his colleagues left the school amid the tears of the students and parents.

He came to the school at the early hours of the morning. The soldiers at the gate did not allow him to enter. There was chaos and confusion. This distinguished hub of education, where they had always inspired peace and education, was turned into a part of a dirty game. Attempts to reach his local friends by phone were in vain. It was as if consciences had gone dumb. Ears had become deaf. "What a pity," he said! "What a pity! They play with the future of so many young people! All the hard work and dedication we put into these schools…" He was so sad and could not hold back his tears. His colleagues had similar feelings of disappointment. The next days were no different than a nightmare. As if the seizure of the school had not sufficed, this time the officials demanded them to leave the country. They issued threats.

About thirty families were shoehorned into two truck-like buses with what little belongings they were allowed. They drove the education volunteers, whom they had cherished and bestowed awards for their achievements until yesterday, like criminals. Like Prophet Yusuf (peace be upon him), the educators could reach Senegal after a 30-hour journey marked with illness, betrayal, and threats.

Mr. Hakan and his family took temporary refuge in the home of a friend in Senegal. During their last days in Mali, they got a cat which had sulked at life after its owners had left for France. They had named their new friend Fındık, who had been abandoned with a wounded leg. They took the cat to the vet and got it treated. Fındık sprung back to life thanks to its new owners. Hakan and his family, meanwhile, shuttled to and from the airport many times and under much hardship to travel to Europe. They spent a lot during this quest.

Finally, they boarded a plane to Europe with three fellow families. Since Turkey had refused to issue them documents such as passports, despite being their most natural citizenship right, they had to experience further problems.

They had moments of fear no different than those in detective novels. Amidst police interrogations, problems with their documents, fears and worries experienced by children as young as babies, they reached Europe safely. They took a deep breath and sought asylum at the airport, out of desperation. They were retained in the refugee compound at the airport for 10 days. They had a hard time, but the caring attitude of the staff alleviated the agony of those difficult days.

Portugal, the Western European country where they sought asylum, is half Europe and half Africa with its sea and humble people. They loved the Mediterranean climate and the loving, warm-blooded people at first sight. The sorrowful days full of adventure they left behind would not be easily erased from their memories. On the first night in their home, Hakan's son Ömer's first question was "Dad, I wonder what Fındık is doing now?" After long procedures that took nine months, they got permission to bring Fındık to Europe from Senegal with substantial costs. Fındık was ecstatic with the joy of having been reunited with his truehearted owners. Mr. Hakan and his family have set sail for new horizons, but what about the pearls of the Black Continent they left behind?

What about those who persecute these teachers who cannot even leave a cat uncared ...?

"You are valuable and beautiful even with your loneliness, failures, inadequacies, and constrictions. You need to escape from life, to prepare for bigger escapes."

*(Sabahattin Ali)*

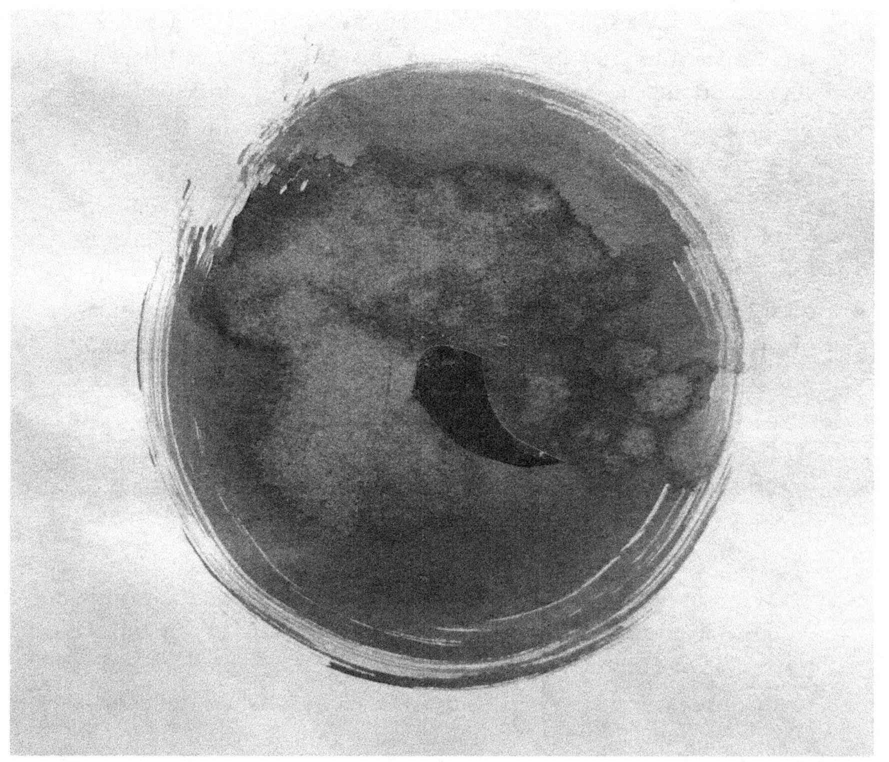

# WAS EMILE ZOLA A TRAITOR?

The justice of an intellectual is measured by raising their voice against injustice, their courage, placing the expression of the interests of their society over their own interests, implementing this as a code of life, and above all their sensitivity to the problems of others as if they were their own. A person who speaks as per the conjuncture cannot be termed an intellectual.

An intellectual has something to express to society in the fields of culture, science, philosophy, and several other disciplines, and who paves the path for them. The responsibility of the intellectual is not to invent weapons of mass destruction, but to prevent or mitigate the damage such weapons cause to society. What makes them into an intellectual is their ability to synthesize the accessible data and information; first internalizing it and then converting it into a healing pill. It is their courage to speak the truth, not just to oppose.

On May 15, 1984, a group of intellectuals wrote a petition in which Aziz Nesin said, "Our beautiful country has been turned into an open-air prison". The intellectuals of that period struggled for democracy. However, some so-called artiste intellectuals withdrew their signatures and quoted eccentric reasons such as "We thought the petition was a letter for public housing".

Having criticized the policies pursued by the French government and army during the German War in his novel "Decadence" published in 1892, Zola became a public hero for defending a Jewish soldier who was wrongfully convicted during the war. Writing his last novel after this incident which went down in history as the "Dreyfus Affair", Zola created the novel's storyline as inspired by the Dreyfus Affair and later converted it into an open letter to the then-President of the French Republic published in the front page of the newspaper, showing a true intellectual sensitivity. He was an intellectual who paved the path for a Renaissance and removed several roadblocks and social pressures. Zola risked death with the article he wrote, but he never stopped telling the truth and defending the right albeit it was not his personal cause. He encouraged numerous intellectuals, growing into a social hero whom intellectuals like Sartre followed as an example and wrote about. He paved the way for the freedom of expression.

Emile Zola's open letter expressing the responsibility of the intellectual. He drew attention to the restoration of justice which had been obscured by saying: "January 1898.

J'accuse! Mr. President, may I tell you, in gratitude for the kindness you showed me one day, that I have only concern for your glory, and that your star, which has hitherto been so fortunate for you, is threatened by the most shameful and ineffective blots? You have come out safely, free from slander, and have conquered hearts. You are radiant with the devotion of this patriotic festival which the Russian alliance has caused for France, and you are preparing to preside over the solemn triumph of our Universal Exhibition, which will crown our great century of work, truth, and freedom. Yet, the Dreyfus affair is disgustingly a mud stain on your name. A council of war, in turn, dared to win Esterhazy for all truth and justice. And it is over; France now has this stain on herself. History will chronicle under your presidency, along with your name, that such a social crime could have been committed in the past. I will dare what Dreyfus dared; I will dare. I will tell the truth, because I promised to tell everything, if justice was regularly seized and if those who should have done it did not do their part. My duty is to speak; I do not want to be an accomplice. My nights are haunted by the spectre of the innocent man whose life ended there, dying under the most horrible tortures. And for you, Mr. President, with all the strength of my rebellion as an honest man, I will shout out this truth. For your honour, I am sure you do not know the truth. And if not to you, O the chief judge of the country, to whom will I denounce the evil swamps of the actual criminals?"

Galileo was likewise punished for speaking the truth, the scientific truths, and was subjected to lifetime house arrest. Meanwhile, he had not done so to contradict the Church, but to express the truth.

There have always been people whose freedoms have been restricted and who have been tortured for speaking the truth. Regimes and dictators who persecute and oppress those who speak and defend the truth have always existed since the establishment of the world order. Thanks to the intellectuals who speak the truth, these regimes of oppression and bloodshed have not lasted long.

Currently, many intellectuals like Ahmet Altan, Sedat Laçiner, Osman Kavala, Selahattin Demirtaş, Gültekin Avcı, Mümtaz'er Türköne, Hidayet Karaca, Mustafa Ünal, Mehmet Baransu, İlhan Çomak and several others have almost been sentenced to death or many years in prisons for writing and speaking the truth.

Many intellectuals like Socrates, Galileo,Fakhruddin Razi, Averroes, Ibn Khaldun, Zola, Muhammad Hamidullah, Fazlur Rahman, Mehmet Akif Ersoy, Nazım Hikmet and Halit Refik paid a heavy price; they were declared traitors and suffered exile. Writer and intellectual Cemal Uşşak, who lost his life in exile, have also taken their places in the shameful exhibits of history.

As long as there are effort and struggle, let's not sink into despair. Let's not look at what is happening instantly, but at what is changing surely.

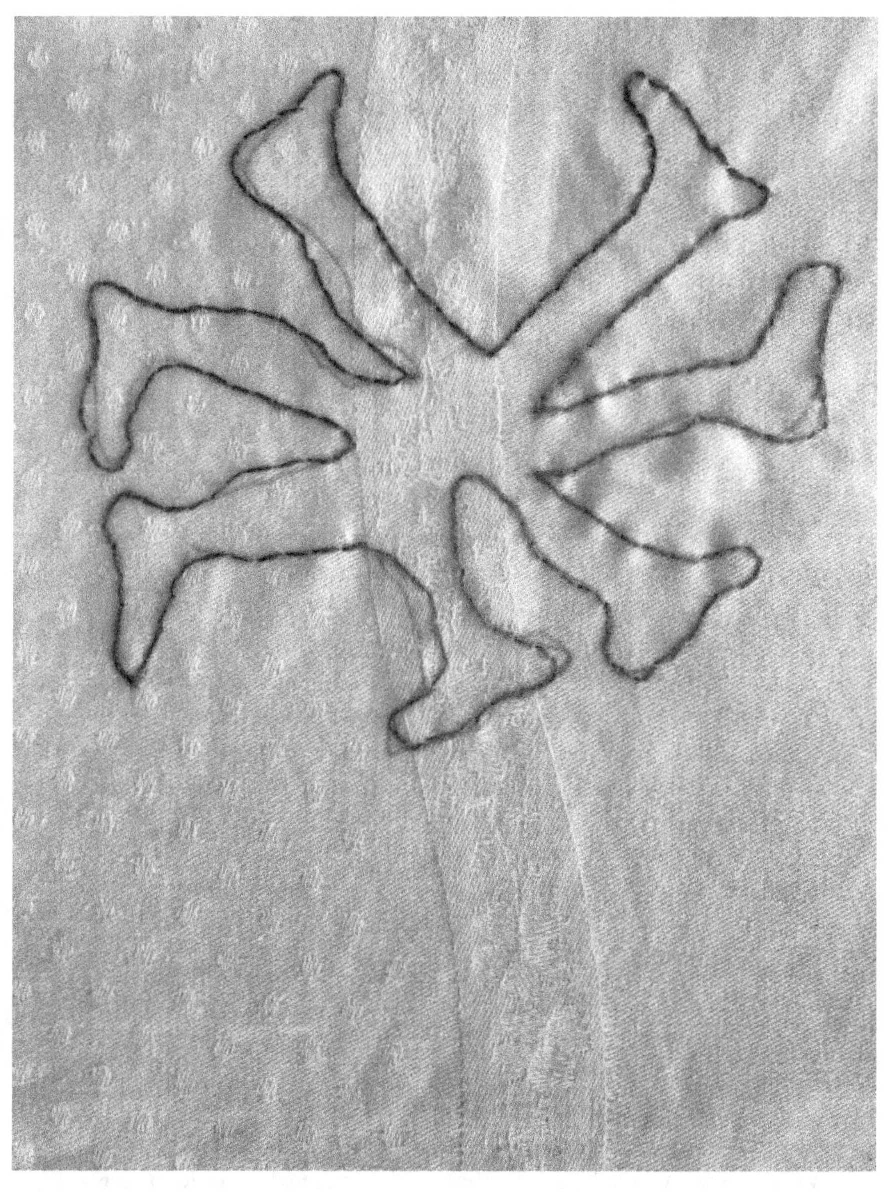

# JUSTICE ON DUSTY SHELVES

**It** is not enough to interpret events and philosophize about them! It is necessary to take pains over how to change them, give them direction, and find solutions.

In 1993, six members of the same family, including an eight-day-old baby, were shot dead in Xirabreşk village of Cizre district. 80-year-old Davut Elgün, who lost his wife and children, stated that the massacre had been covered up despite the testimonies of witnesses and added, "Who should I complain for whom?" Numerous massacres took place in Şırnak and its districts in the 1990s. Some was perpetrated on a deserted street or in a field or in front of everyone in houses burned down and fusilladed with heavy armour. The perpetrators are still not found.

In his article titled "We Are Not Unique", Cevheri Güven wrote "The only assets of the Kurds living in the villages were their houses, fields, and animals. The houses were evacuated and set to fire by the officials. The villagers could not return to their fields for 10 or 15 years. Isn't this a kind of property seizure? And I mean hundreds of villages. This process accelerated so fast in the 90s that the population of Diyarbakır province increased by 1 million in a short time."

Hobbes' Leviathan, the monster state, continues to devour its own children. When they deem minorities or strongly prominent communities like the Hizmet Movement as a threat to countries like Turkey, where democracy has yet to mature, the regime officials continue to persecute and eradicate people. Democracy is for the individual. However, in sacred statist countries, individuals have no value; they can easily be sacrificed for the state. I would prefer a more peaceful and prosperous life summarized as "May the citizens live long" instead of the "May the homeland live long" mindset.

Sufferings, victimizations, and deaths cannot be placed in competition. Each human is a realm and bears unique value. We are humans first and then Muslims or the adherents of other faiths and religions. Our suffering does not constitute a reason for superiority. No rule allows the one who suffers the most to be considered the most virtuous.

When questioned about the agony they suffered in the 80s, the majority of those who had been tortured and suffered in prisons in those years keep silent and do not wish to talk about it. Many people like Aydın Engin or the late Muhsin Yazıcıoğlu either ridicule or keep it a secret to alleviate the agony of the days they experienced. This nation has always concealed its pain and lived with the longing for justice. "But I did not suffer this much for you to take after others as well..." says the late author Cemil Meriç.

Both Nurefşan and Mahir Mete Kul, who disappeared in the waters of Evros River, are our pain and common loss. If Davut Elgün is still seeking justice for his lost family, it does not differ from the struggles of the family of Yusuf Bilge Tunç, who has been missing for years.

Journalist Hrant Dink, another painful loss, used to say that if Turkey becomes democratized, everyone in the country will be able to solve their historical and current issues much more easily. Individuals and states that cannot face themselves and their history are doomed to be crushed and disappear under the treads of history. With oppression, you only produce hypocritical, unethical, unthinking, and unproductive individuals, and one day the system you produce will devour you too.

In this period, when we are rapidly moving towards the days when there is no return of humanity from democracy, let us place a semicolon here with the question "Where does the humanity lead to?" asked to Hegel who replied, "It flows towards a world in which it will be liberated."

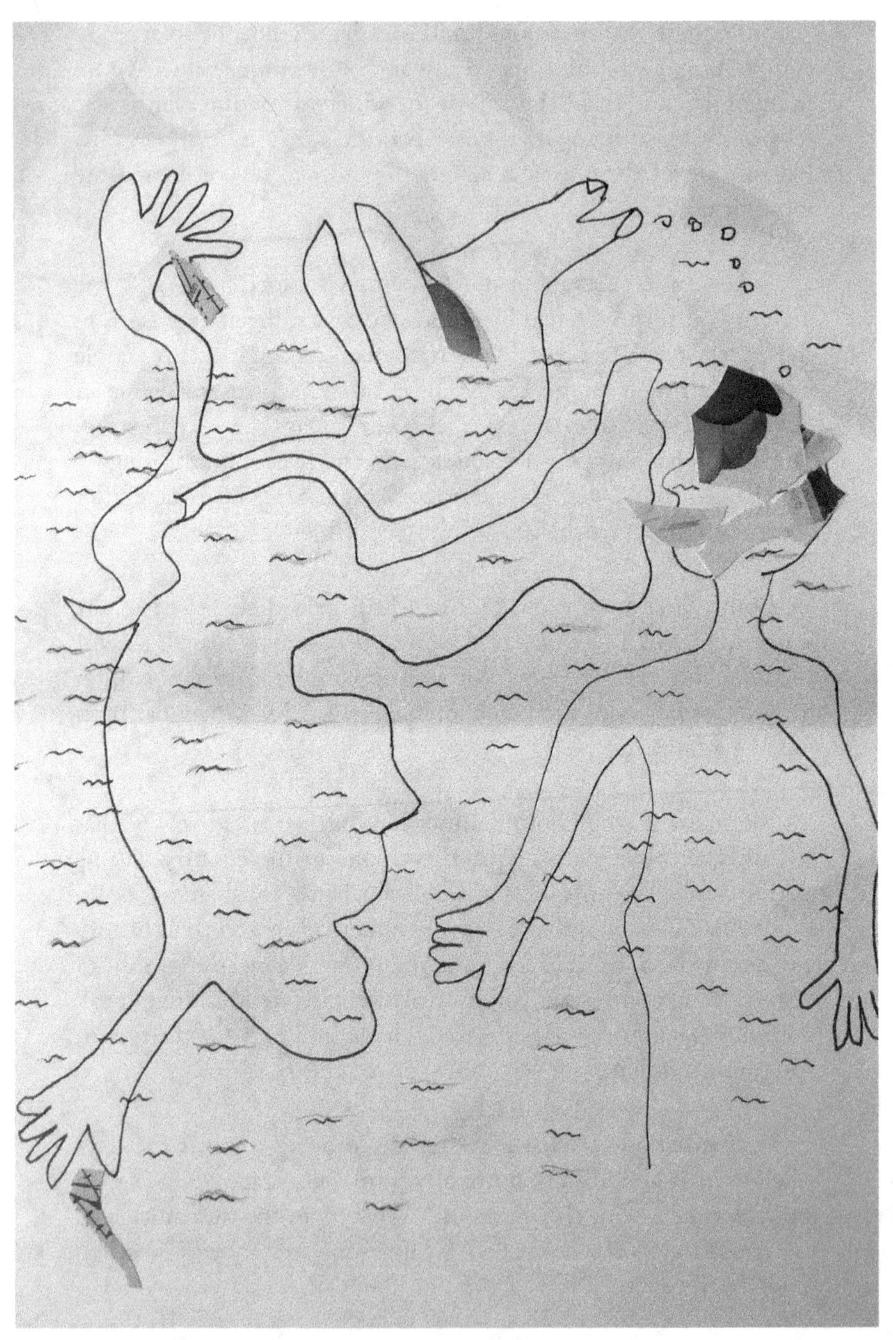

# STOCKHOLM AND OUR INTELLECTUALS

Those who live without thinking are figures of other people's philosophies of life.

I wrote about Silivri and intellectuals. I wanted to add a new one to the adventurous and sad story of intellectuals. My lifetime friend Mustafa, who has been living in Stockholm for ten years, affected me to write this article.

I am listening to composer, writer Zülfü Livaneli: "I was followed like a fugitive, and I had to flee abroad with a fake passport. I took refuge in Sweden and was imprisoned there because I could not prove my identity. I was only saved when my wife and children arrived. I was found guilty in my country because I was Zülfü Livaneli and in Sweden I was guilty because I could not prove that I was Zülfü Livaneli," he says ironically. He makes light of the fact he was declared a traitor and a terrorist by restoring to black humour, saying a man who reads books and plays the saz does not make a

traitor. "I eventually become a member of the Turkish Parliament after being nominated as an Ambassador for Peace and was honoured to a degree when they even granted me a red official passport," he adds with a laugh.

Journalist Yavuz Baydar recently wrote about Demir Özlü, an intellectual who had to flee Turkey to Sweden. Özlü is yet another regime-affected intellectual who left this world on February 13, 2021, leaving behind several literary works.

Stockholm Stories received many awards including the Sait Faik Story Award.

Yavuz Baydar wrote: "If I am not mistaken, I met Demir Özlü

in early 1979. Like every honest Turkish intellectual who was concerned and worried about the course of his country, he received blatant threats during that terrible period and chose to exercise his right to leave Turkey. I would realize much later that the real reason was not about his life, but an immense pessimism – which did not separate him from the right path – through deciphering the profound operating codes of the country."

People with leftist and rightist worldviews continue to exile in Europe and America. Several intellectuals are subjected to exiles similar to those back in the 80s and earlier. In the last six or seven years, many well-equipped intellectuals, journalists, academics, and bureaucrats who now live in Sweden were forced to leave Turkey, no different than the likes of Zülfü Livaneli and Demir Özlü. The systematic witch- hunt conducted by the regime against the participants and sympathizers of the Hizmet Movement continues on a much more violent scale than in the past.

Perhaps due to being the country of the Nobel Awards, Sweden has a charm that attracts intellectuals. I first heard about Stockholm from Ishak Alaton when I listened to his memories. Nowadays, qualified individuals who will be remembered for their literary works, journalistic achievements and activist work on human rights continue to work in Sweden, struggling to survive on the one hand and producing quality work on the other. We have high-achieving intellectuals who hold on to their lives and have produced quality work in Germany, the Netherlands, Belgium, France, England, the United Kingdom, the United States, Canada, and other democratic countries. Chronicles of their lives are already being written.

In such difficult times, those who set goals and accept things as they are, have been able to adopt a more productive and solid stance for the future than those who rely on superficial and idealistic hopes. Those who lose hope and ideals are in danger of falling into a dark abyss.

For today's intellectuals, especially for the children of countries like ours, Cemil Meriç speaks from the past: "The script was penned by others. We were only actors.

Generations had been victimized by a utopia".

When we listen to Cem Karaca's Wait for Me or Ahmet Kaya's Don't Burn [Exile], they show us that similar to different voices and breaths coming from the same source, our pains, hopes and dreams are common and sometimes similar.

Each person whose heart beats for humanity and continues to struggle for the relative goodness to triumph, is a light, radiance, and thought. When the light moves, it pierces the darkness; make no mistake about it.

Let us end with John Locke, a founder of liberalism: "From whatever point of view, the law valid on earth is human, and therefore it can only be established by the consent of the people. Hence, no one can be compelled to obey a law or authority not based on the consent of the people".

# DEATH IN A WHITE PLASTIC CHAIR

Little Elif lying curled up in the court corridor, the little child asking to a dog, "Dog, where's my mummy?" Teacher Gökhan who died writhing in a congested detention room, and finally Deputy Police Commissioner Mustafa Kabakcıoğlu who died in a white plastic chair... 600 lives and souls: each saying goodbye to life with a different tragedy ...

Dismissed from civil service via a statutory order, Mustafa Kabakçıoğlu was imprisoned for four years. He spent the last four months in solitary confinement. He petitioned several times but to no avail. He wailed, "Let this be a lesson for me and a heartache for you. I cannot get my health checks done and I cannot lead a healthy life. May Allah not let anyone be imprisoned here", as if leaving a will.

Mustafa Kabakcıoğlu was a police officer who received a certificate of appreciation from the Ministry of Interior in 2007. He was a patriot who put his life on the line so the nation could sleep peacefully at nights. Like hundreds of his colleagues behind the prison bars...

Our hearts ache for the lives disregarded by indifference and for political interests in our country. Our hearts ache for the indifference of the concerned authorities. One cannot help but dissent against such who lead lives like the blind and the deaf...

This is not the first time these deplorable tragedies have happened, and it will not be the last. While democracy is still a dream, it will surely come to our country one day. The days when people can live humanely and when justice stands by the oppressed and the victimized will surely come. Rights, justice, and freedom will certainly be restored. In countries where justice has shrunk, it is the criminals who roam larger.

Police Commissioner Mustafa, abandoned to die alone in a solitary cell leaving his three children behind, is a snapshot of today's regime in Turkey.

As Alija Izetbegovic said, "All trials are a pale imitation of the Divine Court."

# THE FOUR HEROES

These four individuals are undoubtedly the leading figures who work hard to prevent the perpetuity of the current persecution process:

Ömer Faruk Gergerlioğlu, HDP Member of the Turkish Parliament born in Isparta.

Enes Kanter, NBA player born in Zurich. Melek Çetinkaya, mother of Cadet Furkan. Human rights defender Arlet Natali Avazyan.

Since the coup attempt on July 15, 2016, to 2022, 559,064 people have been investigated under the pretext of the attempt, 261,700 were detained and 91,287 – 780 of whom are babies – have been imprisoned.

129,411 public officials, 150 out of 326 generals in the Turkish Armed Forces, 1,119 out of 1,894 staff officers (59%, of the total personnel) were dismissed for the same reason. 533 people lost their lives.

Mr. Ömer Faruk Gergerlioğlu, who endeavours like a one-man opposition party and parliament, has always stood by the victims and the oppressed. He has given them inspiration and hope. He extended his helping hand to the victims and oppressed people in the remotest corners and stood for them not because of their opinions and views, but because they are humans and are victimized. He faced obstacles but he did not give up. In my opinion, like Nelson Mandela, he struggled and continues to give a struggle for the human rights violations in Turkey. He had the same stance when he chaired the Mazlum-Der (The Association for Human Rights and Solidarity for the Oppressed). History will remember Mr. Gergerlioğlu as the hero who spread his hands wide against Erdoğan and his stooges and exclaimed, "Stop, hordes! This is a dead end!"

Former NBA player Enes Kanter will be remembered as the man who single handedly did the work of hundreds of NGOs and human rights associations and announced the current persecution to the world. He became the voice of those who lost their lives in Evros River, breathed their last in prisons, subjected to tortures, exiled from their homeland, and deprived of their jobs and livelihood. He was disowned and subjected to all kinds of slander but continued to proclaim these atrocities to the world without breaking his stance.

Contrary to many of his colleagues, he did not remain silent about unlawfulness out of fear of ruining his career. He objected to China's persecution of Uyghurs at the expense of jeopardizing his career in the NBA. Enes Kanter has been embraced and chronicled in the United States and the world for his honourable stance.

Melek Çetinkaya – fondly lauded as Melek Anne (Angel Mother) as well –undoubtedly puts up the incredible struggle of being a mother of an oppressed person. No different than a fervent seeker in the scorching desert, she goes from door to door, seeking the rights of her cadet son and his peers.

She does not give up, she does not stop, she does not rest, she does not lose heart ... as one day her struggle will bear fruit and her son, whom she knows to be innocent, will be freed. She even transformed her two-month incarceration into a greatly constructive retreat. She became a source of morale for the inmates, and when she was released, she made a note in history by saying "I have two children outside, and I have 313 children inside. I was happier inside". Mrs. Melek's struggle reminds us of her namesake, Mrs. Melek İpek. Recently, Mrs. Melek Çetinkaya was rejoiced by her son's release from the prison. She endeavours for ensuring the freedom of all unwarrantedly imprisoned cadets.

Human rights defender Arlet Natali Avazyan was born in Malatya. She supported the cause of eight-year-old cancer patient Ahmet Ataç – whom she nicknamed Kara Efem (My Brunet Hero) – until his last breath. She provided all kinds of humanitarian support to this forlorn child and his mother, while the father was in prison, and taught history a lesson in humanity by taking care of the oppressed in these difficult times.

During this period of oppression, the once-unknown accounts of hundreds of thousands of victims and the struggle of the oppressed have undoubtedly been written and will continue to be written. The wails of the oppressed makes the Throne of Mercy tremble.

"Never mind, so be it, for the Creator is the Most Intimate Friend,

Never think the tyrants will get away with what they did, The sigh of the oppressed topples sovereigns,

There surely is a time for everything."

*(Yunus Emre)*

# PEOPLE ARE DYING
# IN MY COUNTRY

People entered 2017 with the agonizing news of dozens of people killed in a brutal and dastardly attack on an entertainment centre in Istanbul. Unfortunately, the tragic incidents we have been reading about in Syria for a long time now happen in my country as well. In recent years, bombings, assassinations, rapes, and murders have intensified as if they were ordinary events and it is saddening to witness our people have gotten used to these.

People are dying trivially in my country. Meanwhile, most so-called media institutions ruthlessly target certain social groups, making the situation even worse by polarizing the society. Terrorists are now running rampant in my country and the law enforcement officers who could have prevented them are mostly in prison. Ours is the very country that imprisons the most journalists in the world. Judges, prosecutors, academics, and highly successful businesspeople are imprisoned or forced to flee abroad.

Ours is the only country which ventures through the state apparatus to close the private educational institutions opened abroad.

Ostensibly religious folk have monopolized the religion. They expect the religion to be practiced as they say. The space allotted to the non-religious people shrink daily. In my country are monsters who have no pity for the people killed while celebrating the New Year's Eve, who say the victims deserved their end and that it is nice they were killed.

Religion has been turned into the most dangerous weapon. People are driven away from the religion and made to hate it. Religious institutions compete in immorality. Violence and hatred pervade society from all sides.

We were not like this. Marginalizing, targeting, and beating the fallen did not exist in our world. We used to be a tolerant society. There were days when we lived with love without interfering with people's beliefs. We could become a peaceful society. We could become hearts beating as one against our enemies.

Renaissance will happen again once we revert to our national and spiritual values. Yet, these values cannot germinate and grow in a climate of hatred, anger, and envy. Especially if you lump honest and honourable people who have never passed a police station in their lives with monsters like the ISIS militants who bluster they represent Islam through terror and atrocity, and if you criminalize the innocent with all kinds of crimes and slander, believe me, neither in this world nor in the Hereafter will you make ends meet. You will be doomed to live in constant frustration and downfall.

# THE EPIC OF
# ESMA ULUDAĞ

**M**rs. Esma Uludağ's tragedy is a mini map of these years of persecution. It is an interpreter of what hundreds of thousands of people have gone through. If there had been no other persecution, what she and her family had gone through would have come enough as sin and shame for the ruthless people who caused it.

Imagine a woman who graduates from two universities as a mother of three children, qualifies as a government employee, and never stops learning. 32-year-old Esma Uludağ graduated from Dokuz Eylül University, Department of Physics in 2007. In 2009, she began graduate studies at Celal Bayar University. Meanwhile, she got married and became a government employee. Finally, she enrolled in Gediz University Vocational School of Justice. She graduated from Gediz University Vocational School of Justice as the top scoring student. She received her diploma with her three children, one of whom was only 38 days old, and took wings with her love for education and determination to have education. While working at the Karabağlar District Governor's Office, she continued her education.

The fearful days arrived with severe pressures. Treacherous attacks were launched on a life dedicated to human life and love. She was accused of crimes which even did not cross her imagination and sent into prison. She suffered the dispiriting pang of separation from her children down to her bones. After three months, she was released on probation which required her to sign her attendance at a police station regularly.

Her husband Mr. Mehmet Ali had left for Germany some time earlier. Mrs. Esma, dismissed from the civil service via a statutory decree issued under the State of Emergency, crossed the

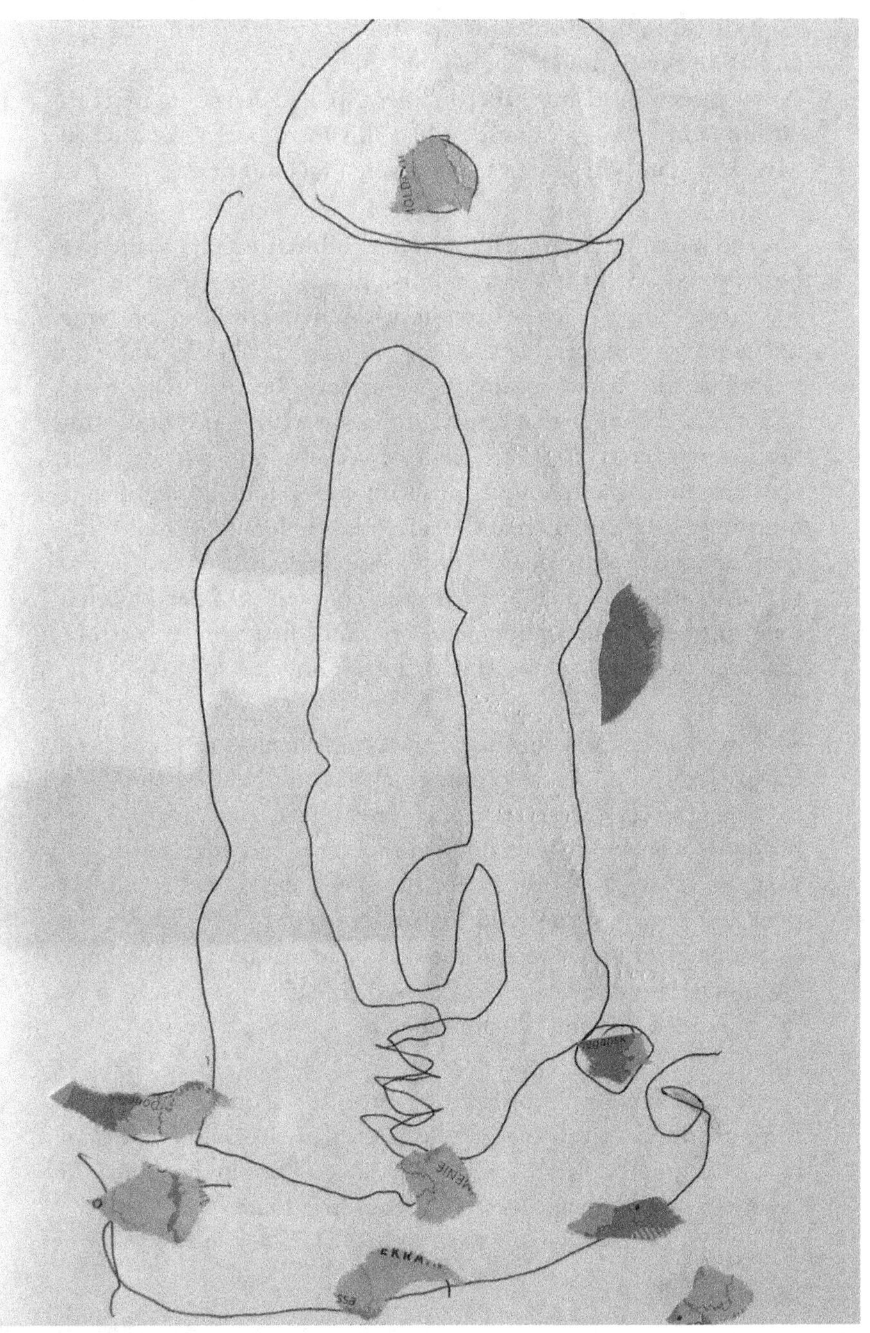

Evros River under great hardship with her cute children aged 3, 7 and 10 in tow. After an hours-long ordeal of travel, they reached Greece. Her husband Mr. Mehmet Ali had been granted his family reunification request. When this fortunate news reached Mrs. Esma and the children, they were on cloud nine.

The longing had peaked, and the children eagerly waited to be reunited with their father. Mrs. Esma, on the other hand, was profoundly worn out from imprisonment condition, leaving her country and her loved ones, crossing the border through an ordeal, the harsh conditions of asylum, burden of longing, and stress. Having an excruciating wait with the longing for her husband and the excitement of reunion and with so little time left until the reunification, Mrs. Esra suddenly fell ill one morning. They called an ambulance and took Mrs. Esma to the hospital as her teary-eyed children watched with worry. It was the last time she could see her cute children and her children their mother. In the ambulance, Mrs. Esma first suffered a stroke and then breathed her last due to a heart attack.

Mr. Mehmet Ali could arrive in Greece thanks to an expedited travel permit, but he could only reach the see the lifeless body of his wife. The children greeted their father with tears, saying "Our brave dad's back!" as tears flooded their eyes and angels watched over the scene. This was an epic ... which dealt heavier impact than any previous one; nothing more, nothing less. This is the story of a great ordeal reciprocated with a great reward. My hope and prayer are that those who caused this tragedy must be held to account in this world before they die.

We can have no words and wishes for those who stepped forth as innocent towards the horizon of their souls other than to say, "Enjoy the Paradise and be patient a little longer, you will experience eternal happiness with your loved ones".

# THE GOLDEN GENERATION ÖZCENGİZ

*Venue: Çorum Conference Hall*

It is 1977. The hall is full of young people from different provinces. The orator Fethullah Gulen is in his 30s and delivers a profound and effective lecture. The subject is "The Characteristics of the Golden Generation" which our country has been longing for centuries. The orator enthusiastically talks about love, action, and self-account ... He emphasizes unity and solidarity and says suffering ordeals is an indispensable part of the mission. He talks about the inner and outer conquests and quotes vivid examples from the time of the Companions of the Holy Prophet (PBUH).

*Venue: Çorum Prison*

It is 2019. Muzaffer Özcengiz has been held in solitary confinement for 14 months without medication or care for his requests. He has been in prison for two years. He is a religious studies teacher. He submitted petition after petition asking the officials not to take away his right to life, but no one pays attention. From the top to the bottom, they fell on deaf ears; even the most notorious terrorists do not receive such treatment. This cannot be defended in any humanitarian or legal sense. In 2015 alone, 426 people perished in prison and the names of those who caused these deaths are on record.

I have known Muzaffer Özcengiz since 1995 or so from Izmir. He remained in my memory with his kindness, gentlemanliness, and his righteous and valiant personality. He was the director of the Uğur Student Dormitory for Boys. He would receive the visitors with a cordial attitude and make great efforts to raise the Golden Generation, the ideal youth in a disciplined and diligent manner. He would visit one shopkeeper after another to request scholarships for the boarding students and so he would meet their needs. Who knows, he possibly had students from those who currently persecute him ... He was a patriotic and conservative person who loved his country.

Muzaffer Özcengiz was one of the last people in life to be labelled with terrorism. Yet, even so, he was imprisoned for 2 years and 14 months in solitary confinement without access to lifesaving medication. The volume of his prescribed medications increased four-fold. At the last visit, he clutched his wife's hand tightly, as if he did not wish to part, and looked into her eyes for a long time.

Today's cruel rulers thus reciprocated for his service to this country and the youth by being depriving him of his heart medications. During his last days, he could no longer breathe easy and had lost mobility almost completely.

Indeed, the Golden Generations came into being. While they lived on that ideal and devoted themselves to the ideal of keeping it alive, they themselves became the Golden Generations. They showed how to aspire to suffering by sacrificing their lives. They stood firm against the oppressors of the era and passed away from this world by crowning their eternal lives with martyrdom. They marched to the horizon of their soul by leaving behind a life lived Companion-like as an example to the future generations and their children.

The fate of people like Muzaffer Özcengiz are the symbols of this century of oppression. It is also proof that the likes of Muzaffer Özcengiz, who listened to that orator that day in 1977, and the Golden Generation came into being.

# A MARTYR OF EDUCATION: GÖKHAN AÇIKKOLLU

Gökhan Açıkkollu is a 42-year-old history teacher who was killed in police detention under torture without understanding why and without being proven guilty...

Teacher Gökhan, a history teacher at the Ümraniye Atatürk Technical and Industrial Vocational High School in Istanbul, was taken into custody from his home on July 23, 2016, in the wake of the dastardly July 15 coup attempt. He had dreams and he was in love with his profession. He was a role model teacher, much loved by his students. He was a family man. His cute children waited with fond eyes for their father to arrive in the evening. He was exemplary with his lifestyle; he was also a faithful educator and an enlightened person.

When they took him into custody, the officials first called his wife and she arrived at the police station in a hurry. She was curious and worried, "What kind of crime could a teacher have committed to justify his custody from his residence at midnight?" What kind of a treatment was this for a teacher known by everyone including the parents at the school and who was a paragon of honesty? The family returned home distraught and helpless.

Teacher Gökhan suffered 14 days under torture. He was diabetic, but his medication was delivered to him. For days and long dark nights he kept on thinking, "What have I done for this country and the youth other than serving them?" ... He watched his family and children with his mind's eye and tears welled up in his eyes. He was aware he had paid a price for this country like millions of others. Finally, his feeble body and slender soul could not bear this heavy burden any longer. He breathed his last leaving behind disillusionments and longings. He ewas martyred and alone in a hospital corner, sensing only the presence of his Lord, but forlorn.

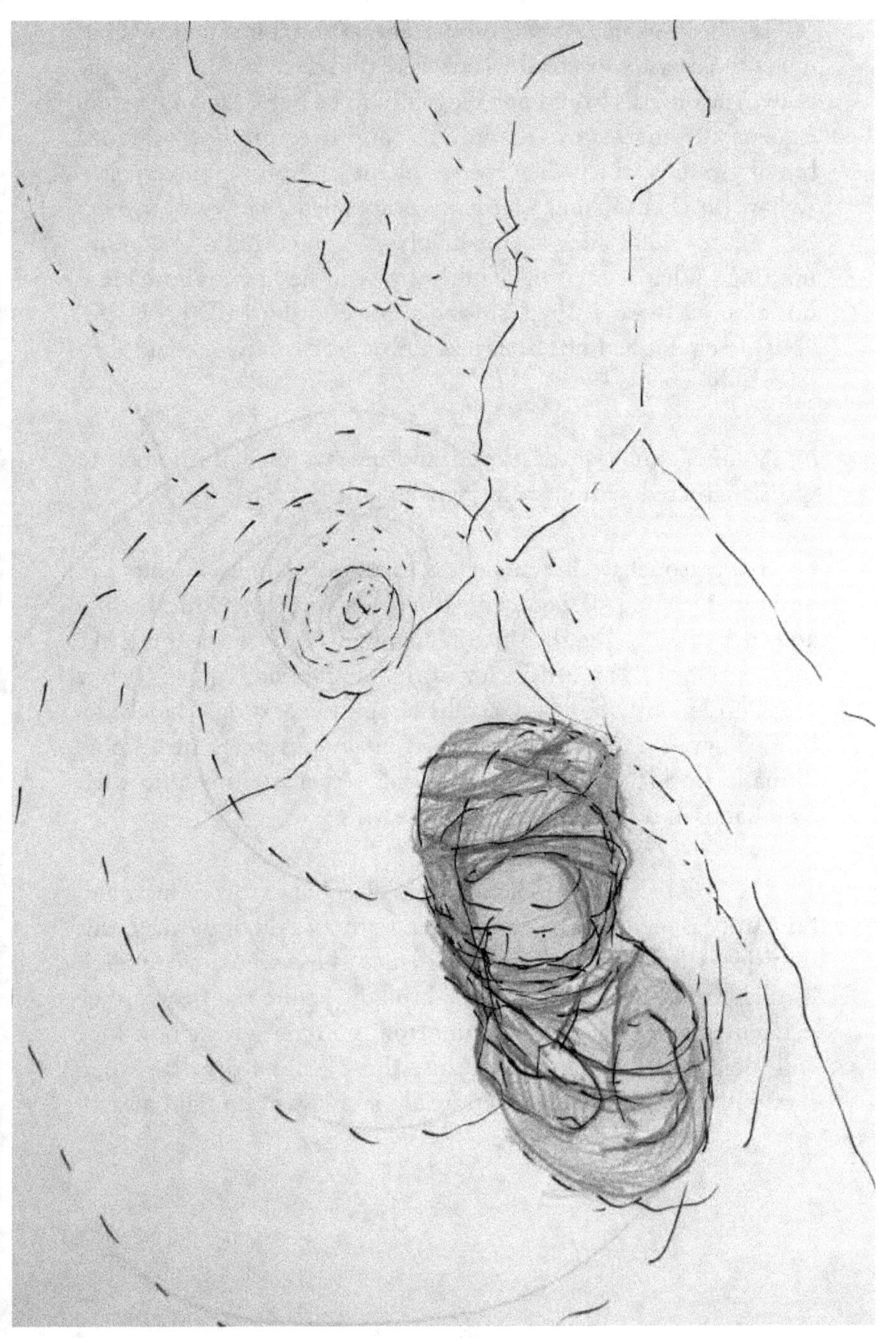

Teacher Gökhan's family received news from him after days, but it was the news of his death. They were told to come and claim the body. The officials would not allow him to be buried in an Istanbul cemetery. In the wake of the July 15 coup attempt, they fashioned burial grounds which they termed as the Traitors' Cemetery. Mr. Ayhan, Teacher Gökhan's father, was appalled. "How can my son be a traitor while he was not involved in anything and commit nothing? What is my son's fault? How can he be a traitor? He is not allowed to be washed, shrouded, or even buried!" he wailed. "His statement had not been taken even in custody," he said with tears in his eyes.

Another family was destroyed, and another son of the homeland was slaughtered without being proven guilty.

If a person has chosen such a mission for himself, they can never be accused of betraying their country, its political unity and social peace. The rhetoric of 'anyone who does not think like me is a traitor' is an evil legacy of the totalitarian regimes. A free mind is obviously opposed to official opinion and rigid blockades of ideology. Yet, such minds wish to make possible a freer, more humane world in which everyone takes their destiny into their own hands and faces the consequences.

The likes of Teacher Gökhan are as essential to this country and humanity as medicine, air, and water. In this world or the next, this injustice will be exposed sooner or later. Those who are complicit in this persecution today will be brought before the people they persecuted and their families tomorrow. I am not saying how they will look them in the face, because those will be the days when they will say "Wish the ground would swallow us up right away!"

# IDEAS CANNOT BE KILLED

Pangea means supercontinent, from the Greek pan (whole) and gaia (earth). This notion was proposed by the German scientist Alfred Wegener in 1912. Pangea, the ancestor of all continents, has a 335-million-year history.

Albeit diverse opinions, our story as humans' dates back 300,000 years. At the beginning of the human story are emotions like violating prohibitions, love, embarrassment, jealousy, and revenge. In Goethe's master opus Faust, which he wrote in 60 years, is the pain and effort of a young scientist who attains the pinnacle in several fields of science, then admits himself as an unenlightened person who knows nothing, stops giving lectures and attempts to reinterpret existence. The novel tells the story of his journey to rediscover existence and truth. Doctor Faust is confronted by Mephisto who tries to lead the young Faust astray with all his evil skills.

Actually, as humanity, we have never run out of our periods of surprise. Nights have brought us days, wars have brought peace, winters have brought springs, and global epidemics have brought us further cautious days with new ways of treatment and prevention. Fascism, ultra-nationalism, and anti-immigrant discourses are on the rise. Migration from war zones to safer harbours continues. Autocratic regimes become objects of hatred thanks to the likes of Putin and Erdoğan. People seek new ways out because of these authoritarians' aggressive, disregarding others, completely pragmatist, conscience-less, human-less projects and egoistic attitudes. They build new lives in new worlds. An integration across humanity is underway, while brand-new consensuses are established. The struggle between good and evil, between Faust and Mephisto continues unabated. Global and universal stories of humanity are coming to life with our individual stories.

Mehmet Ateş, a cardiac surgeon, is a scientist who has broken records worldwide with his techniques and has been discussed in international science journals. A day comes and he is declared a terrorist in his own country. He is hounded nook and cranny, his assets are seized, his hospital is shuttered, he is separated from his family, his freedom is taken away and so the list goes on. Yet, Mehmet Ateş MD is as fiery as his surname in Turkish, and he does not give up his struggle. Even if they put him in prison and deprive him of his basic human rights, he does not give up. He somehow flees abroad. He continues to practice his values and ideals in his host country. He struggles to endure in the health sector through his new endeavours in medical science. Meanwhile, he writes research articles and provides earnest support to the quest of justice as an activist against human rights violations.

We are all saddened by the heartrending end of Ekrem Karakaya MD, who was murdered recently. Still, I do not know if those do not raise their voices for hundreds of thousands of high-achieving and virtuous professionals dismissed from public employment via statutory decrees and have been marginalized and excluded for years can now observe the pit of hatred and anger Turkey country has reached and its consequences. Professionals in several fields including healthcare leave Turkey in desperation or undergo severe depression and traumas. Not everyone is Mehmet Ateş MD; not everyone can go abroad or can express the same level of resilience and strength. However, the current situation is heartbreaking and depressing for our country. A huge country has been thrown into the fire for the lust of some for power and wealth. The deadly silence and the masses who remained silent have also become partners in this shame.

Our stories constitute the stories and history of humanity. Tens of thousands of people like Mehmet Ateş MD building brand new lives both in Turkey and abroad in different countries. They do not surrender to Mephisto; they continue to produce and hold on to life. Despite everything, they stubbornly continue to love and say, "neither the moment nor the agony endures." No true ideal or cause can be terminated by oppression and tyranny. True ideals and causes do not or cannot end when their frontrunners pass away.

"Ideas and thoughts embraced by the world and humanity cannot be killed; rather, they take wings and roam the world." - Averroes

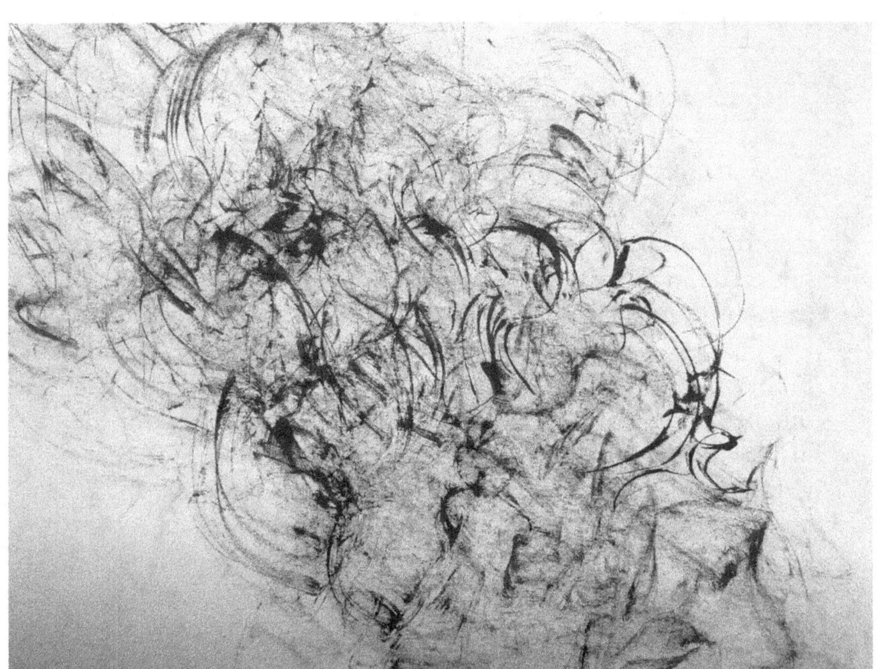

# VICTIMIZATIONS EMBROIDERED IN BELGIUM

"**I** find art meaningful when it includes human beings. Art exists to express people's suffering. In the pushbacks is no hospitality, no human rights! Then what is left?"

*Dutch artist and performer, Nell Berger.*

Awareness activities are regularly held in Europe and the United States to announce the victimizations in Turkey. Most recently, Solidarity with Others organized the #StopPushbacks project to raise awareness and form public opinion on push backs in Europe. On Sunday, March 6, 2022, an art exhibition was held to raise awareness about the pushbacks of refugees at Europe's borders. In this context, three Dutch artists shared with the public the stories of people subjected to push backs for the first time through a performance and exhibition. Evros River virtually transformed into a dragon on the way to the beloved. The shores of Greece are like steep mountains to overcome.

They have been the hub of several ordeals and human tragedies. Humanity buries its pain and shame in Greek soil and on the banks of the Evros.

The inhuman treatment and especially the imprisonment, torture and severe traumas suffered by the Hizmet Diaspora, the Gülen Movement and the Kurds in Turkey through pushbacks have been recorded in the history of humanity as exhibits of shame. These tragedies were woven into fabrics in Belgium as well. Stitch by stitch, these experiences were embroidered into hearts. With this artistic action in downtown Brussels, a subtle but resonant message was given to Europe and all humanity:

"O humanity! If you have not lost your conscience, support all people who have become refugees and whose human rights have been taken away, without discriminating them in race, religion, or colour! You can make your voice heard to the world through the language of art."

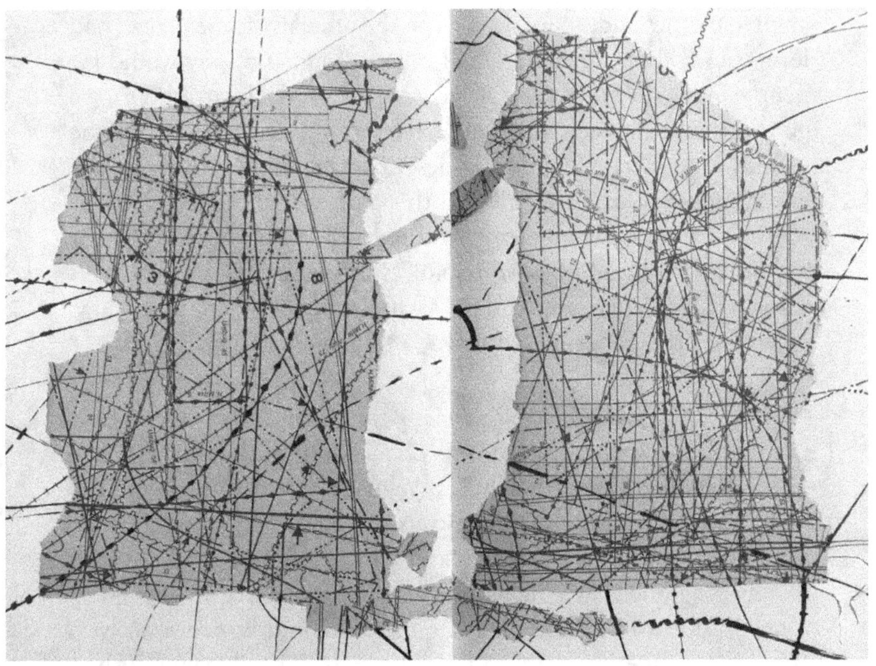

The story of a father and son who crossed into Greece and marched for freedom at the risk of their lives in the darkness of the night was immensely touching to make consciences bleed. The father, who tied money in place of the cotton his son took from a farmland on the way, reminded us of a scene we are familiar with from the honourable past of our ancestors. This memorable painting was embroidered on the fabric as if to engrave it in the memory of humanity.

Mr. Hasan's story is so heartrending: "They forced us down on our knees and placed the barrels of their pistols to the back of our necks, subjecting us to humiliating treatment. Later, they loaded us in a hardtop vehicle with only a spare tire in the back. I and my friend had trouble breathing. We started kicking the vehicle as we were about to die... They opened the door again to let us breathe and took us to a place which I think was a police station. They merged us in a group of about 40 people, including African migrants, and loaded us on a large boat. There were people in civilian clothes and ski masks next to the officials. These people had long sticks, about one and a half meters long, and they would hit people indiscriminately and force us to get on the boat. And so, we got on the boat. They dumped us back to the Turkish side for the second time. Mrs. Hüsniye too described the moments of fear she experienced: "Our experience on this path we set out for freedom was agonizing. I was physically and psychologically exhausted. For a month I had nightmares of soldiers in black masks at night. It was so difficult for me to dare to flee abroad again. Even now, when I see the police here, I worry and panic so much.

Mrs. Derya, another pushback victim, recounts with tears how they were insulted, cursed, put on boats, and pushed back to the Turkish shore: "It was the end of August, so we had expected the weather to be warm. However, it was ice- cold everywhere. Finally, we realized the earth was warm and we started digging. It seemed like digging one's own grave... As we dug, the hot earth came out. Once in every 15 minutes we dug the earth and buried ourselves. We took refuge in Allah and the hot earth until dawn. When it dawned, we looked for a way out. We tried to get out of the marshland for about two hours; meanwhile, my husband sank in the marshy ground, and we struggled to get him out. It was hard. Our freedom was completely taken away from us, and it hurt us a lot to receive such treatment from Greece, the country we took refuge in. What we went through is weighs heavy on us, even now my voice trembles when I talk about it. I do not wish others to go through the same. We thought a lot about going abroad again, about crossing to Greece, about our freedom. There was nothing we could do; we had no means to live in our own country."

Notwithstanding nationality, the common denominator of the people forced to leave or flee their home country is being refugees and victims. Europe should embrace all who have been subjected to war, dictatorship and persecution like Ukrainians, Syrians, and Afghans, and protect them on equal terms. The victims' identity cannot be questioned.

# QUESTIONING THE VICTIMS' IDENTITY

Our anger, greed and jealousy make all evils commonplace. This lies beneath all what is happening in Turkey and the irresponsible and oblivious lawlessness of the oppressive regime. Unending hatred, anger, oblivious greed, insatiable selfishness, jealousy, and a sense of inadequacy…

Statements like "Republic is the rule of the virtuous" or "Republic is virtue" or "Sovereignty belongs to the nation unconditionally" do not go beyond slogans; actions and discourses do not match. In today's Turkey, it is easy to find examples: What an oddity is it to sentence Murat Arslan, the chair of a prominent judicial organization like YARSAV (Turkish Association of Judges and Prosecutors) and the winner of the Vaclav Havel Human Rights Award, to 10 years in prison for insulting the President?

How can one explain the imprisonment of Rector Prof. Sedat Laçiner, one of Turkey's most important strategists and youngest professors, a scientist who was awarded the Young Global Leader Award by the Davos Economic Forum, and who authored dozens of books and hundreds of international articles?

What kind of outdated mentality is it to try Ali Ünal, a valuable scholar who in my opinion authored one of the best Qur'anic commentaries in Turkey and perhaps in the world and authored one of the English meaning translations of the Qur'an, who reminds us of the Companions of the Holy Prophet (PBUH) through his virtuous life, and who authored dozens of books, with three life sentences?

What kind of a sheer contradiction is it to keep an activist like Osman Kavala, who has made a name for himself in the business world and who carried out significant works in defence of human rights, in prison despite the ECtHR rulings?

We can give hundreds of such examples. A mindset that tries Turkey's best journalists, academics, businessmen, members of the judiciary, security forces and military personnel on superficial and trumped-up grounds and abandons them rot in prison is anachronistic. As Mümtaz'er Türköne says, "If there is no judiciary, there is no constitutional order."

Let us quit questioning the identity of the victim; instead, let us fight oppression on the side of the victims. So-called intellectuals, the intellectuals who remain silent about these incidents, and those who profile victims for their identity bear massive shame. Those who confine themselves in the exclusive echo chamber of their own social group are always lacking. Tomorrow, they should not walk around introducing themselves as intellectuals and artistes of this country, and no one should believe those who are dead-silent today!

Europeans are sensitive about human rights violations. When they are informed especially in their own countries and when they meet in person and listen to your story of victimization, they are more sensitive than many of our own fellow citizens. A judge I visited recently expressed his sorrow after listening to the human rights violations in Turkey. I realized he knew much more than what I told him. He criticized the illegalities in a humorous way because no solemn explanation could explain them. I also observed him making earnest serious efforts to eliminate these grievances. The world is actually aware of everything; silencing and manipulating the media and the judiciary can only provide a temporary false happiness in your country, but you cannot silence the world. Especially when the morphine wears off, it is inevitable to face the truth and pain.

Periods of persecution serve as quality litmus tests, facilitating you to observe the events like from an observatory. Stars and fireflies come out in the open. We observe how small the so-called great "artists", glorified by people with praises as "father" or "doyenne" of their fields can become, and we are disappointed. Writer Emine Eroğlu says, "The most prominent indicator of being an intellectual is fearlessness. It is not being afraid of death, isolation, or exile. It is not to be articulated to power." It hurt to observe those who have become lapdogs of power and the lickspittles of the Palace; yet it also revealed the truth, for how much of a price or prize did they sold themselves. It turned out it was actually a thin curtain which covered the shameless faces. Meanwhile, the events also brought to light the true heroes and intellectuals who cannot be bought and sold and introduced brand new role models to humanity.

Because "things necessary are never said in excess, and truths are never said in vain. The word, even if it does not prevail, shows that truth is eternal."

*(Stefan Zweig)*

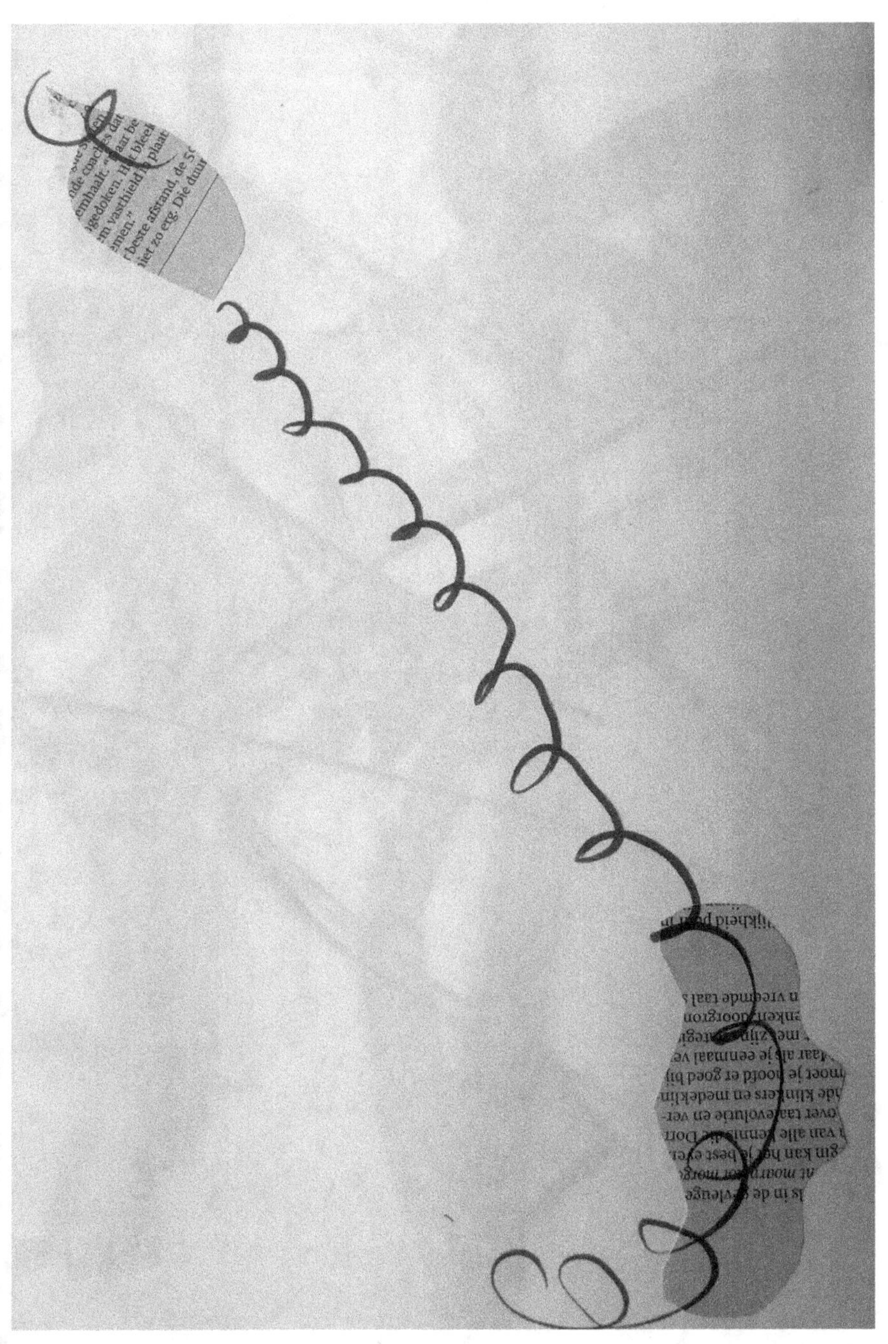